& THEIR FAVORITE FLOWERING PLANTS
BUTTERFLIES
Anza-Borrego Desert State Park® & Environs

East San Diego County, California
Desert, Chaparral, Montane

Painted Lady sipping nectar at Brittlebush

Anza-Borrego Desert State Park® and environs as defined here encompass the entire eastern watershed of San Diego County, California—desert, chaparral, montane. This area includes all of the State Park. The western border is the steep eastern slope of the Peninsular Range as it plunges to the desert below. The eastern border is the Imperial County line. The northern border is marked by the northern boundry of the Park (slightly into Riverside County) and the southern border extends to Mexico.

Dedication

To the volunteers of our area who serve to interpret and preserve its natural wonders by working with the Anza–Borrego Desert State Park®, the Anza–Borrego Desert Natural History Association, the Anza–Borrego Foundation and the San Diego Natural History Museum Canyoneers. These volunteers first sparked our curiousity about San Diego County's rich flora and fauna.

Acknowledgments

Many thanks to Anza–Borrego Desert State Park® Superintendent Mark Jorgensen and to Colorado Desert District Resource Ecologists Paul Jorgensen and Jim Dice for their encouragement and for access into new Park acquisitions not yet open to the public.

We are indebted to Dr. Paisley Cato at the San Diego Natural History Museum and to Collections Manager Virginia Scott at the University of Colorado for assistance and the use of their collections.

Thanks also to the authors of the many helpful publications on butterfly and plant biology, and to several mentors and friends who generously shared their knowledge with us. Greg Ballmer, John Emmel, David Faulkner, Jeff Oliver and Paul Opler provided useful discussions and assistance in identifying caterpillars, caterpillar food plants or butterflies. Ken Osborne furnished us with his butterfly records of the Mason Valley area migrants and strays. Craig Reiser identified many caterpillar food plants for us and guided us to their locations. James Scott identified several of the caterpillars. Ray Stanford sorted out some very difficult skippers. And especially, Gordon Pratt shared with us his vast knowledge of California butterflies, their caterpillars and food plants and patiently answered a multitude of questions. Our gratitude to all of you.

Published by Merryleaf Press
13780 N. Saint Vrain Dr.
Lyons, CO 80540-9034

Printed by Lorraine Press, Salt Lake City with Agfa CristaRaster stochastic screening and vegetable inks on acid free 100# Sterling Ultra Gloss Text with 10% recycle content

ISBN # 0-9615125-2-0
Library of Congress Number 2003113738

A GRANITE RIDGE NATURE BOOK

Our Mission: *To interpret the natural world, emphasizing insects and their plant relationships, through field studies and research in order to further scientific knowledge and to instill and inspire in the general public an acquaintance, awareness and appreciation of all nature.*

CONTENTS

Introduction

Butterflies & their Favorite Flowering Plants

Species Accounts

A Quick Guide to the Butterfly Families
Anza–Borrego Desert State Park® & Environs

SWALLOWTAILS (PAPILIONIDAE)

Large, colorful and conspicuous; usually with tail-like projections on hindwings. (7 species)

'Desert' Black Swallowtail

WHITES & SULPHURS (PIERIDAE)

Mainly white, yellow or orange; often sparsely marked with black. (19 species)

Becker's White

California Marble

Sara Orangetip

California Dogface

Subfamily: WHITES (Whites, Marbles, Orangetips)
(PIERINAE)

Most have white uppersides with a few black markings; some have orange tips. Undersides are white to gray with darker (sometimes green) veins or marbling. (8 species)

Subfamily: SULPHURS
(COLIADINAE)

Yellow, orange, sometimes whitish, with black borders. (11 sp.)

COPPERS, HAIRSTREAKS & BLUES (LYCAENIDAE)

Small, dainty; brown, orange, gray, purplish, green or blue; some with metallic luster. When wings are closed over the back, often perform "hindwing rubbing." (39 species)

Great Copper

Leda Ministreak

Sonoran Blue

Subfamily: COPPERS
(LYCAEINAE)

Upperside brown with a coppery or purplish sheen; underside gray-white; dark markings on wings. (4 species)

Subfamily: HAIRSTREAKS
(THECLINAE)

Most are gray or brown; often with hair-like streaks on the underside and hair-like tails on hindwings. (17 species)

Subfamily: BLUES
(POLYOMMATINAE)

Upperside metallic blue in male, often brownish in female; underside gray-white with dark spots. (18 species)

METALMARKS (RIODINIDAE)

Small, orange and/or brown with dark markings; some have white spots; some have attractive rows of silvery metallic spots paralleling wing margins. (5 species)

Wright's Metalmark

BRUSHFOOTS (NYMPHALIDAE)

Mainly medium-sized in shades of browns, oranges, yellows and blacks. Front legs of both sexes are small, brush-like and not used for walking. (28 species)

American Snout

Coronis Fritillary

Leanira Checkerspot

Subfamily: SNOUTS
(LIBYTHEINAE)

Small, brown-orange with white spots; mouthparts (palps) project like a nose. (1 species)

Subfamily: LONGWINGS
(HELICONIINAE)

Mainly orange with dark veins and markings; some with large silver spots on the underside. (4 species)

Subfamily: TRUE BRUSH-FOOTS (NYMPHALINAE)

Diverse in color and pattern, but mainly hues of brown, orange and black. (17 species)

California Ringlet

California Sister

Monarch

Subfamily: SATYRS
(SATYRINAE)

Camouflage shades of gray, brown, orange or yellow; eyespots along underside wing margin; prefer grassy, shaded habitats. (2 species)

Subfamily: ADMIRALS & RELATIVES (LIMENITIDINAE)

Handsome with a contrasty pattern of black, white and orange; found in riparian areas with oaks, willows, chokecherries. (2 species)

Subfamily: MILKWEED BUTTERFLIES (DANAINAE)

Brightly colored orange to reddish brown with black and white markings. (2 species)

SKIPPERS (HESPERIIDAE)

Most are small with stout, hairy bodies and relatively short wings resembling some moths; head and eyes are large; colors of orange, brown, gray or blackish often with whitish spots; most with antennal club bent backwards; darting flight. (34 species)

White Checkered-Skipper

Western Branded Skipper

California Giant Skipper

Subfamily: SPREAD-WINGS
(PYRGINAE)

Often sit with wings spread wide open unlike the other two skipper subfamilies; colors of brown, black, gray and white. (18 species)

Subfamily: GRASS SKIPPERS
(HESPERIINAE)

Often sit with hindwings spread more open than forewings; shades of brown, gray, orange; underside may have spots or patches. (14 species)

Subfamily: GIANT-SKIPPERS
(MEGATHYMINAE)

Stout body, small head, no hook on antennal club unlike other skippers; often sit like Grass Skippers with wings partially spread. (2 species)

5

Butterflying in our Area

Butterflying is the popular and pleasurable pastime of observing and identifying butterflies in their natural environment. It is akin to birding. Already many visitors travel to Anza-Borrego Desert State Park® to enjoy the displays of spring flowers. This book hopes to enrich that experience by helping you find and identify the colorful butterflies so often associated with flowers.

Gray Hairstreak on Rock Hibiscus

Butterflies and plants are intimately entwined, having evolved together over millions of years. Butterflies rely on specific plants as food for their caterpillar offspring. Also, most butterflies sip flower nectar for nutrients and moisture.

An outing to observe wildflowers can be expanded to include looking for and observing the array of intriguing butterflies in myriads of colors and in sizes ranging from tiny, dainty and jewel-like to large and flamboyant. It's hard to convey the enthusiasm, the excitement, the joy of each new butterfly discovery, the pleasures amplified by seeing them nectaring at showy blossoms, the satisfaction of learning each butterfly's name and so making the acquaintance of a new friend. Like birders butterfliers often use binoculars, especially close-focus models, as aids for viewing pattern details.

Our sunny area with varied habitats ranging from low desert to chaparral to pine-clad mountains includes a fantastic range of flora, plus 134 recorded species/subspecies of delicate solar-powered butterflies, about one out of six of the nearly 800 butterflies found in the United States and Canada (almost 17%).

Why such a local butterfly book? Across the country there are many look-alike species. A regional book includes only species occurring in the area, making their identification simpler. It can guide you to habitats and locations where you are apt to see certain species. This book also includes photographs of area food plants for each caterpillar species and of favorite nectar flowers adults visit (a total of 147 plant species).

How to Use this Book

Of the 134 butterflies pictured in this book, the 118 butterflies you are more apt to encounter are arranged by families, with closely related or similar species displayed together. Also included are photos of 16 additional migrant or stray species.

Beneath each butterfly's common and scientific name are two "**vital statistics**" :

(1) **Size in inches,** measured with wings open from forewing tip to forewing tip. Butterflies may be **tiny** ($1/2$"–1"), **small** (above 1"–$1\frac{1}{2}$"), **medium** (above $1\frac{1}{2}$"–$2\frac{1}{4}$") or **large** (larger than $2\frac{1}{4}$"). Butterfly photos are enlarged beyond life size so as to show detail.

(2) **The months the butterfly** *may* **fly** based on California early/late records (Stanford *et al*, 2002), depending on sufficient rain and when the rain occurs and on elevation. Butterflies fly earlier at lower than at higher elevations. Some species have one (1) flight per year lasting a month or two, other species have two (2) or several (sev). Semi-tropical species fly off and on all year.

Each butterfly species is described and illustrated with one photograph or more. Following this is a section on the plant(s) its caterpillars eat in our area with at least one food plant pictured. Sometimes caterpillars, eggs and/or chrysalises are shown.

How to Find Butterflies? By Habitats & Habits

Most butterflies do not fly everywhere. They fly where their needs for habitat, food, moisture and habits are met. Below are some guidelines for locating butterflies.

- *Butterflies prefer different habitats.* The Tiny Checkerspot flies only where its caterpillar food plant Chuparosa grows, mainly in sandy desert washes. The Painted Lady whose caterpillars eat many plants is cosmopolitan. To find the most butterfly species, look in different habitats. Our region is rich in varied habitats: deserts, canyons, chaparral, mountains. See the Habitat Chart and Map on pp. 8–9.

- *Butterflies fly at different times of the day.* Some fly early in the morning, some prefer mid-day, and some fly more often or only in the afternoon.

- *Butterflies fly at different times of the year.* Desert Orangetip flies only in the spring. The California Giant-Skipper flies only September to October. Many butterflies have a limited season. Others fly much of the year.

- *Look for butterflies in different years.* In arid areas such as ours where yearly rainfall varies dramatically, so does butterfly abundance. Some butterflies will delay their metamorphic cycle for one or more years unless rain is adequate.

- *Look for butterflies nectaring on wildflowers,* especially on perennials and on flowering shrubs and trees that tend to bloom reliably year after year.

- *Look for butterflies around water.* Many butterflies, especially males and often in groups, sip mud and wet sand for moisture, salts and trace elements (puddling).

- *Look for male butterflies searching for females.* Males of some species, called **perchers,** sit on a plant or on the ground waiting for a female to fly by. Other males, **patrollers,** fly back and forth along canyons, washes or trails. Butterflies of some species rendezvous at the highest **hilltops.** Here the males perch or patrol, and unmated females seek romance by flying up to the hilltop.

- *Look for the caterpillar food plants.* Butterflies concentrate around these plants. Here the female lays her eggs. Males may perch on the plant or be nearby awaiting females. At times you may find an egg, caterpillar or chrysalis on these plants.

- *Look for butterflies basking in the sun.* Butterflies are cold-blooded. In early morning or on colder days they bask to warm up. Some species bask with wings spread wide. Other species bask with closed wings held perpendicular to the sun's rays for maximum solar radiation.

California Sister sipping Yerba Santa   *Western Tiger Swallowtail sipping wet sand*

7

Selected Butterflying Locales

ELEV. FEET	MAP	LOCATION	HABITAT	TYPICAL PLANTS
	CD3-4	BORREGO SPRINGS	RESIDENTIAL / AGRICULTURAL	CITRUS, LANTANA
	F3	COACHWHIP CANYON	BADLANDS	DESERT HOLLY, ORCUTT ASTER
	CD3-4	BORREGO SPRINGS VALLEY	CREOSOTE BUSH SCRUB	CREOSOTE, BURROWEED
	D3	HENDERSON CANYON RD - EAST	DUNES & MESQUITE HUMMOCKS	SAND VERBENA, MESQUITE DUNE EVENING PRIMROSE
	D4	PALM CANYON DR - EAST		DESERT DICORIA
	D4	BORREGO SINK	ALKALI SINKS	SALTBUSH, SALTGRASS
BELOW 1500	BC3	BORREGO PALM CANYON	DESERT SUCCULENT SCRUB (ALLUVIAL FANS STEEP ROCKY SLOPES)	CHOLLA, BARREL CACTUS OCOTILLO, DESERT AGAVE INDIGO BUSH
	BC4	HELLHOLE CANYON		
	D5	SENNA WASH		
	F3	COACHWHIP CANYON / ELLA WASH	DESERT MICROPHYLL WOODLANDS (SMALL LEAF TREES IN DESERT WASHES)	DESERT LAVENDER DESERT WILLOW CATCLAW MESQUITE IRONWOOD DESERT SENNA SMOKE TREE CHUPAROSA CHEESEBUSH
	BC2	COYOTE CANYON-LOWER WILLOWS		
	BC3	BORREGO PALM CANYON		
	BC4	HELLHOLE CANYON		
	D5	SENNA WASH		
	B5	BITTER CREEK CANYON		
	C5	PLUM CANYON		
	BC3	BORREGO PALM CANYON	DESERT RIPARIAN (PALM OASES, SPRINGS, CANYONS)	DESERT FAN PALM COTTONWOOD CA SYCAMORE IRONWOOD, MESQUITE MULEFAT, FALSE INDIGO
	BC4	HELLHOLE CANYON		
	C5	YAQUI WELL		
	E9	MOUNTAIN PALM SPRINGS		
1500 - 3500	BC4	CULP VALLEY / UPPER TUBB CANYON	DESERT TRANSITION (INCLUDES PLANTS OF BOTH DESERT & CHAPARRAL)	DESERT APRICOT SCRUB OAK DESERT JUJUBE CALIFORNIA JUNIPER TURPENTINE BROOM SUGARBUSH DESERT DUDLEYA DESERT AGAVE MOJAVE YUCCA NOLINA
	B4	MONTEZUMA VISTA POINT		
	C5	PLUM CANYON		
	B6	SAN FELIPE / SCISSORS CROSSING		
	AB5	SAN FELIPE VALLEY - BLM		
	BC7	BOX CANYON		
	E11	JACUMBA AREA		
	BC4	CULP VALLEY / UPPER TUBB CANYON	DESERT TRANSITION RIPARIAN	WILLOW, COTTONWOOD MESQUITE YERBA MANSA MULEFAT, NETTLES FALSE INDIGO
	B6	SAN FELIPE / SCISSORS CROSSING		
	B6	SENTENAC CIENEGA		
	B7	ORIFLAMME CANYON - LOWER		
+3000	A4	RANCHITA - WESTERN AREA	OAK WOOKLAND	INTERIOR LIVE OAK CANYON LIVE OAK
	A6	BANNER / BANNER GRADE		
+3500	B7	ORIFLAMME CANYON - UPPER	CHAPARRAL (CHAMISE & MIXED)	CHAMISE CEANOTHUS SCRUB OAK MANZANITA MOJAVE YUCCA
	B8	KWAAYMII POINT		
	B8	GARNET PEAK		
	A2	COMBS PEAK		
+4000	D7	WHALE PEAK	PINYON-JUNIPER WOODLAND	PINYON PINE, CA JUNIPER
	B8	GARNET PEAK	MONTANE CONIFEROUS FOREST	JEFFREY & COULTER PINE BLACK OAK CA INCENSECEDAR
	A2	COMBS PEAK		
	A7	CUYAMACA LAKE AREA	MOUNTAIN MEADOWS	GRASSES, SEDGES, RUSHES HERBACEOUS PLANTS
	B8	LAGUNA MEADOWS		

Habitat and plant information adapted from R. Mitchel Beauchamp, *A Flora of San Diego County, California*. 1986.

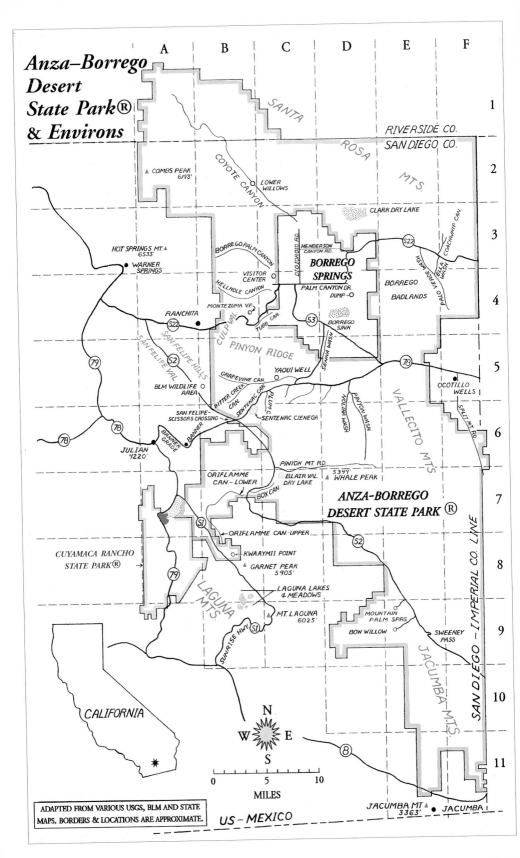

Anza–Borrego Desert State Park® & Environs

A B C D E F

1
2
3
4
5
6
7
8
9
10
11

SANTA ROSA MTS.

RIVERSIDE CO.
SAN DIEGO CO.

▲ COMBS PEAK 6193'

LOWER WILLOWS

COYOTE CANYON

CLARK DRY LAKE

S22

PALO VERDE WASH
ELLA WASH
COACHWHIP CAN.

HOT SPRINGS MT. ▲ 6533'

● WARNER SPRINGS

BORREGO PALM CANYON

HELLHOLE CANYON

VISITOR CENTER ○

DIGIORGIO RD.

HENDERSON CANYON RD.

BORREGO SPRINGS

PALM CANYON DR.
DUMP →○

BORREGO BADLANDS

RANCHITA ●

S22

CULP VAL.

MONTEZUMA V.P.

TUBB CAN.

S3

BORREGO SINK

SEMNA WASH

SAN FELIPE VAL.

SAN FELIPE HILLS

PINYON RIDGE

79

S2

BLM WILDLIFE AREA ○

GRAPEVINE CAN.

YAQUI WELL

BITTER CREEK CAN.

SENTENAC CAN.

TUNE CAN.

SENTENAC CIENEGA

MOLINA WASH

PINYON WASH

VALLECITO MTS.

S78

OCOTILLO WELLS ●

SPLIT MT. RD.

78

JULIAN 4220'

BANNER GRADE

BANNER

ORIFLAMME CAN.-LOWER

BOX CAN.

PINYON MT. RD.

BLAIR VAL. DRY LAKE

5349'
▲ WHALE PEAK

ANZA-BORREGO DESERT STATE PARK ®

SAN DIEGO - IMPERIAL CO. LINE

S1

ORIFLAMME CAN.-UPPER

S2

CUYAMACA RANCHO STATE PARK® →

79

○ KWAAYMII POINT

▲ GARNET PEAK 5905'

LAGUNA LAKES & MEADOWS

LAGUNA MTS.

▲ MT. LAGUNA 6025'

MOUNTAIN PALM SPRS. ○

BOW WILLOW ○

SWEENEY PASS

JACUMBA MTS.

SUNRISE HWY.

S1

CALIFORNIA

✳

N
W E
S

0   5   10
MILES

8

US – MEXICO

JACUMBA MT. ▲ 3363'   ● JACUMBA

What is a Butterfly?

Butterflies like other insects have six legs. In some families the front pair is shortened and not used for walking. They have two pairs of wings, forewings and hindwings, two clubbed anntennae and a long elastic straw-like proboscis for sipping flower nectar, moist sand, mud, fruit juices, sap, dung or carrion.

Its Four Stage Life Cycle—Metamorphosis

- **The Butterfly—Reproductive Stage.** The butterfly is the winged sexually mature adult stage of an insect with a four stage life cycle—egg, caterpillar (larva), chrysalis (pupa), butterfly (adult). Male butterflies search for mates. Mated female butterflies search for suitable plants on which to lay their eggs.
- **The Egg—Embryonic Stage.** Females of most species lay and glue one isolated tiny egg at a time on the food plant. Some species lay eggs in clusters or haphazardly. Egg texture, shape and color are unique to a subfamily or even to genus or species.
- **The Caterpillar (Larva)—Eating and Growing Stage.** The tiny caterpillar, born to eat, hatches. As it eats and grows, its non-expandable skin becomes too tight and splits to reveal a new, larger skin. Each of these growth stages or instars is repeated four or five times. Instars may vary in appearance. Caterpillars hatching from a cluster of eggs usually feed together during early instars, then disperse as they need more food.
- **The Chrysalis (Pupa)—Transformation Stage to the Butterfly.** The caterpillar changes into the chrysalis. Some species pupate on leaves or twigs of their food plant or buried in litter at the plant's base. Other species wander away seeking a sheltered spot. Inside the chrysalis the caterpillar metamorphoses into an adult. The emerging butterfly splits the chrysalis and pumps body fluid through the veins of its limp furled wings to expand and harden them. In about an hour the adult is ready to fly.

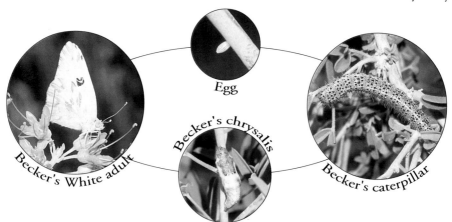

Egg

Becker's chrysalis

Becker's White adult

Becker's caterpillar

Butterfly Life Cycle

- **Number of Flights and Lifespan.** Some butterfly species have a life cycle with one flight a year, while other species may have two or more flights a year. Although most individual butterflies live only a week or two, a flight lasts for several weeks as adults mate and females lay eggs. The rest of the year is spent as egg, caterpillar or chrysalis. One stage (depending on species) is a resting or overwintering stage (diapause). The few species that overwinter in the adult stage may live several months.

Butterfly Color & Pattern

How are butterflies able to display such intricate and colorful wing patterns? **Wing scales** are the answer to this fascinating question. The wings are made of two transparent membranes pressed together to form one sheet. Overlapping rows of tiny scales like roof shingles cover both sides. Anyone who has handled a butterfly knows this coating of scales rubs off easily as a dust with loss of the color pattern.

Each scale is a tiny flat blade, roughly rectangular and about 0.1 x 0.05 mm in size. A stalk on one end of the scale attaches into a socket on the wing. The scale is hollow except for supporting braces and, if present, granules of pigment of only a single color. The wing pattern, like a mosaic tile pattern, arises from the color and arrangement of these scales. Sometimes physical structures of the scale (ridges, thin plates, braces) cause so-called structural colors by the interaction of light with these microscopic features. In some butterflies, both pigment colors and structural colors combine to give the final hue.

Left: *'Henne' Variable Checkerspot showing pigmented wing scales* Right: *A magnified view of a portion of the upperside hindwing showing individual scales,* 170 X

Pigment Colors. Pigments, the most common source of wing color, are chemicals that occur as discrete granules inside a scale. Only one kind of pigment (color) occurs in any one scale. Pigments cause color by the selective absorption and reflection of different wavelengths of white light. Most scale pigments belong to four chemical categories: melanins (black, gray, brown, tan); ommochromes (brown, yellow); pterins (white, yellow, red) and flavonoids (white, yellow).

Structural Colors. Some butterflies display particularly brilliant metallic-like colors. These colors are not due to pigments, but rather to the physical structure of the scales. All butterfly scales have microscopic structures such as ridges and thin plates. To produce structural colors, these structures must have a regular, repeated arrangement and spacing so that white light will interact with these structures to give what is called constructive interference. This optical phenomenon may involve either thin-film interference or diffraction.

We see thin-film interference colors in soap bubbles and oil films on water. We see diffraction effects when looking at the fine regularly spaced grooves of a music CD at an angle. Also, some scales scatter light by pores or granules to give a Tyndall blue, similar to blue sky from light scattered by atmospheric particles, or give a white with a pearly or silvery metallic luster. The blues, greens, coppers and silvery whites of butterflies are structural colors. Sometimes the colors are iridescent, changing

Silvery Blue male displaying structural color

from green to blue and vice versa, for example, depending upon the angles of view and light. Many other creatures such as birds and beetles also display structural colors.

Butterflies & Plants

Relationships

Butterflies require plants at certain stages in their life cycle. To survive and grow, all our caterpillars (immature butterflies) must dine on plants, whether it be on their stem, leaf, bud, flower and/or fruit. And, most adult butterflies obtain nourishment from flower nectar. This book emphasizes these dependent relationships by including information and pictures of the various plants the different caterpillar species eat and the favorite nectar flowers of the adult butterflies.

Nomenclature

Each butterfly and plant species has a common name plus a unique two-word italicized scientific name, the **genus** (plural **genera**), always capitalized and the **species**, never capitalized. If a geographically isolated species population develops distinctive characteristics or appearance, it may have a third name, the **subspecies**.

Classification

Butterflies are classified into the order **Lepidoptera** (meaning Scaly–winged) along with the tenfold more numerous moths. All plants in this book are classified as **Angiosperms** (Flowering Plants) save for two species of **Gymnosperms** (Cone-Bearing Plants). A **species** is a genetically identifiable population of butterflies or plants that are unique and can reproduce themselves. Different **species** believed to be closely related are then grouped into a **genus**. **Genera** are grouped into **families**, with large families divided into **subfamilies**. (To simplify butterfly identification, learn to recognize our six families. See **A Quick Guide,** pp. 4-5.)

Examples of a Butterfly & a Plant Classification

'Henne's' Variable Checkerspot (*Euphydryas chalcedona hennei*)

Kingdom:	Animalia (Animal)
Phylum:	Arthropoda (Jointed Legs)
Class:	Insecta (Insects)
Order:	Lepidoptera (Scaly-winged)
Family:	Nymphalidae (Brushfooted Butterflies)
Subfamily:	Nymphalinae (True Brushfoots)
Genus:	*Euphydryas* (Checkerspots)
Species:	*chalcedona* (Variable Checkerspot)
Subspecies:	*hennei* ('Henne's' Variable Checkerspot)

Woolly Indian Paintbrush (*Castilleja foliolosa*)

Kingdom:	Plantae (Plant)
Division:	Anthophyta (Angiosperms)
Class:	Dicotyledones (Dicotyledons)
Order:	Scrophulariales
Family:	Scrophulariaceae (Snapdragon Family)
Genus:	*Castilleja* (Indian Paintbrush)
Species:	*foliolosa* (Woolly Indian Paintbrush)

Common names of the butterflies used in this book mainly follow the North American Butterfly Association *Checklist & English Names of North American Butterflies,* 1995. All scientific plant names follow Hickman, 1993.

Butterfly scientific names are always subject to revision, especially now with new techniques for genetic and biochemical studies. Authorities often disagree on nomenclature. The scientific names in this book mainly follow Opler & Warren, 2002. In some cases both the scientific name now in common usage and a newer or older one are given.

12

Caterpillar Food Plants

Female butterflies are great botanical sleuths. It is imperative for her offsprings' survival that the female choose an appropriate plant on which to lay her eggs since most caterpillars are finicky and will eat only a closely related group of plants, sometimes only a single species! She finds plants by "tasting" them with tiny sensory hairs at the end of her feet that test for precise chemicals in her caterpillar food plants.

Why are caterpillars so choosy? Because flowering plants and insects have evolved together in an ancient and continuing arms race. Plants (eaten by caterpillars and other insects) have developed an arsenal of chemical defenses including distasteful, bitter, astringent or even toxic substances (such as alkaloids, glycosides or tannins) whose only function seems to be to repel insects.

In return most caterpillar species evolved able to tolerate a few chemicals, usually those common to a specific plant group. Most caterpillar species feed on a few plants of one or two plant families. A few eat plants of several families. No species feeds on all plants promiscuously.

The Wright's Metalmark caterpillar, very choosy, eats only Sweetbush in the Sunflower Family

Of our 118 caterpillar species/subspecies: 101 species feed on plants in only 1 family
11 species feed on plants in only 2 families
3 species feed on plants in only 3 families
1 species feeds on plants in only 4 families
1 species feeds on plants in only 6 families
1 species feeds on plants in only 7 families

For extensive listings of butterflies and their caterpillar food plants, see "Butterflies & their Caterpillar Food Plants" (pp. 106–113) and "Caterpillar Food Plants & Butterfly Species" (pp. 114–122).

Those few caterpillar species able to tolerate particularly noxious plants may specialize by feeding only on them. Twin benefits are: little competition for food and the ability to become toxic themselves to repel predators. The classic examples? Queen and Monarch caterpillars eating toxic milkweeds are toxic themselves.

Caterpillars of all 118 butterfly species/subspecies in our area (not including migrants and strays) eat about 140 species of plants in only 32 different plant families out of a total of 92 conifer and flowering plant families listed in *Plants of Anza Borrego Desert State Park* by D. Clemons, 1986.

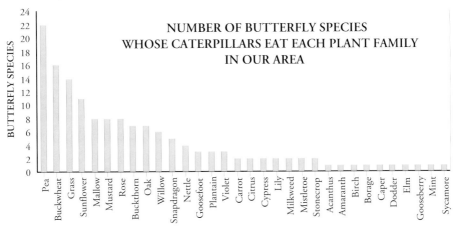

NUMBER OF BUTTERFLY SPECIES WHOSE CATERPILLARS EAT EACH PLANT FAMILY IN OUR AREA

BUTTERFLY SPECIES

Pea, Buckwheat, Grass, Sunflower, Mallow, Mustard, Rose, Buckthorn, Oak, Willow, Snapdragon, Nettle, Goosefoot, Plantain, Violet, Carrot, Citrus, Cypress, Lily, Milkweed, Mistletoe, Stonecrop, Acanthus, Amaranth, Birch, Borage, Caper, Dodder, Elm, Gooseberry, Mint, Sycamore

THE 32 CATERPILLAR FOOD PLANT FAMILIES

13

Favorite Butterfly Nectar Flowers

Most butterflies drink flower nectar, a sugar water enriched with organic substances such as amino acids and vitamins, for nutrition and moisture. In our arid area nectar favorites tend to be reliable shrubs and wildflowers that bloom most years in spite of little rain. We have recorded butterflies sipping nectar from 79 different species in 35 plant families with 30 of these species in one Family, the Sunflower.

Favorite flowers attract the most butterflies and the most species. Early spring butterflies especially favor Desert Lavender, Desert Apricot, Bladderpod, Sweetbush, Spanish Needles and Narrowleaf Goldenbush. Later spring to summer butterflies flock to Buckwheat and Mulefat, fall butterflies to Alkali Goldenbush and Butterweed.

TWENTY NECTAR FAVORITES

Pictured in order of preference. Captions include:
• Months of major bloom depending on rainfall and elevation. Some may bloom again after summer rains.
• Plant's habitat: Desert (D); Desert Transition (DT); Chaparral (C); Riparian (R).
• Number of butterfly species we have observed nectaring on the flowers.

DESERT LAVENDER
Hyptis emoryi
Mint Family
Jan–Apr   D,DT   18 species

BUCKWHEAT
Eriogonum fasciculatum
Buckwheat Family
Mar–Oct   DT,C   17 species

MULEFAT
Baccharis salicifolia
Sunflower Family
Mar–Jul   R   15 species

ALKALI GOLDLDENBUSH
Isocoma acradenia
Sunflower Family
Aug–Nov   D,DT   14 species

DESERT APRICOT
Prunus fremontii
Rose Family
Feb–Apr   DT   13 species

BUTTERWEED
Senecio flaccidus var *douglasii*
Sunflower Family
Jun–Oct   D,DT   13 species

DESERT ARROWWEED
Pluchea sericea
Sunflower Family
Nov–Aug   R   10 species

SWEETBUSH
Bebbia juncea
Sunflower Family
Jan–Jul   D,DT   10 species

14

 Sara Orangetip

SPANISH NEEDLES
Palafoxia arida
Sunflower Family
Oct–Apr   D   9 species

PARISH'S VIGUIERA
Viguiera parishii
Sunflower Family
Jan–Jun   D,DT   9 species

BLADDERPOD
Isomeris arborea
Caper Family
Jan–Dec   D,DT   9 species

DESERT PINCUSHION
Chaenactis fremontii
Sunflower Family
Mar–May   D,DT   8 species

 Painted Lady

FERNLEAF PHACELIA
Phacelia distans
Waterleaf Family
Mar–Aug   D,DT   8 species

NARROWLEAF GOLDENBUSH
Ericameria linearifolia
Sunflower Family
Mar–Jun   D,DT   8 species

 Bramble Hairstreak

DEERWEED
Lotus scoparius
Pea Family
Feb–Aug   D,DT,C   6 species

 Funereal Duskywing

CATCLAW
Acacia greggii
Pea Family
Apr–Jun   D,DT   6 species

SUGARBUSH
Rhus ovata
Sumac Family
Mar–May   DT,C   5 species

SAWTOOTH GOLDENBUSH
Hazardia squarrosa
Sunflower Family
Jul–Oct   C   5 species

FIDDLENECK
Amsinckia tessellata
Borage Family
Mar–Jun   D,DT   5 species

 Checkered White

JACKASS–CLOVER
Wislizenia refracta
Caper Family
Apr–Nov   D   5 species

15

Butterfly Conservation

Butterflies and other wildlife are being pushed out of their habitats by human activities and need our help. Right here in our area, two butterflies are federally listed as endangered species threatened with extinction: the Quino Checkerspot *(Euphydras editha quino)* and the 'Laguna' Two-banded Checkered-Skipper *(Prygus ruralis lagunae).* Some efforts to promote butterfly conservation are listed below.

Xerces Society. This organization, named for the first butterfly in America known to become extinct as a result of human activities, the Xerces Blue *(Glaucopsyche lygdamus xerces),* began butterfly conservation in America in 1971.

North American Butterfly Association (NABA). Founded in 1992 to promote butterflying as a recreational, non-collecting activity like birding as well as to promote education and conservation. Annual 4th of July Butterfly counts, started by the Xerces Society in 1975, are now run by NABA with volunteers across North America monitoring the various species and their numbers. Since 1997 we have conducted a yearly NABA butterfly count in the Borrego area.

The Sonoran Arthropod Studies Institute. Located in Tucson, AZ, it fosters appreciation of all nature through the vital role arthropods (insects and their relatives) play in the Sonoran Desert ecosystem, which includes the Colorado Desert in East San Diego County, California.

Monarch Watch. Started in 1991 at the University of Kansas to promote science for school children by studying the Monarchs' fall migration with tagging and rearing of Monarchs as part of this activity.

U.S. Endangered Species Act. Since 1973 this act provides for conservation of threatened and endangered wildlife. About 30 insects are on the list of which 20 are butterflies (with 14 of these in California and two of them in our region).

California Endangered Species Act. Overseen by the California Department of Fish & Game, this act parallels the federal act with a petition process available for listing an endangered species. An endangered species is defined here as a species or subspecies of wildlife that is in danger of becoming extinct throughout all or a significant portion of its range.

Butterfly Gardening

Become a conservationist! Anyone with a plot of land can encourage butterflies to visit and even live in your yard. Most adult butterflies sip flower nectar and all of the caterpillars need certain species of plants to eat. Also, many butterflies like to sip moisture from damp sand or mud. By providing some or all of these resources, you can attract and help conserve these beautiful creatures. Two aids for planning your butterfly garden are:

Fiery Skipper visiting Lantana

1. The National Wildlife Federation program called *Backyard Wildlife Habitats.* (www.nwf.org)

2. Butterfly gardening books such as *Butterfly Gardening, Creating Summer Magic in Your Garden,* 1998, by Xerces Society & Smithsonian Institute.

BUTTERFLIES
Anza-Borrego Desert State Park® *& Environs*

Swallowtails (PAPILIONIDAE)

Swallowtails are the most impressive butterflies you will see anywhere in America. They range worldwide, but mainly in the tropics. The 29 species found in the U.S., which occur mostly in our southern states, are divided into two subfamilies. All seven swallowtails found in Anza-Borrego Desert State Park® and environs are members of the **SWALLOWTAIL SUBFAMILY** (PAPILIONINAE).

Pale Swallowtails sipping wet sand

DESCRIPTION & HABITS:
* Large and showy, cloaked mostly in colors of yellow, black or cream.
* Hindwings have long tails resembling those of swallows, thus, the family name.
* Strong fliers using few wing beats per second, flying fairly high overhead.
* Feed at flowers with the unique habit of hovering with wings fluttering.
* Drink at mud and wet sand, sometimes in groups.
* Males of most species patrol for females, but some prefer to perch to await mates.

PLANTS EATEN BY THE CATERPILLARS: Food plants eaten by our species include the following families: Birch, Buckthorn, Carrot, Citrus, Rose, Sycamore and Willow.

Eggs: Eggs are globe-shaped, smooth with little or no texture and greenish to cream depending on the species, all with brown markings. They are laid singly on the food plant.

Caterpillar (larva): All species are smooth-skinned with colors, depending on the species, ranging from white to green to black with colorful markings or brown with a white pattern resembling bird droppings. Of special interest is the osmeterium, a bright orange or yellow horn-like structure unique to swallowtails. It is usually not visable, but can pop out from a slit behind the head to release noxious chemicals for repelling predators such as ants, wasps and flies.

Chrysalis (pupa): Protectively colored brown or green. The posterior end is attached to a button of silk, spun on a branch or other support, by tiny hooks called the cremaster. A girdle of silk across the middle supports the pupa upright.

Hibernation: The chrysalis is the over-wintering stage. Some swallowtails may remain in the chrysalis stage for more than one year. The 'Desert' Black, the Anise and the Indra Swallowtails probably use this survival strategy in drought years in our area.

'DESERT' BLACK SWALLOWTAIL
Papilio polyxenes coloro

Size: Large (2¼"–3⅛")   *Flies:* Feb–May; Sep–Oct if summer rains (1–2 flights)

'Desert' Black Swallowtail seeking refuge from wind on Desert Apricot

The 'Desert' Black Swallowtail, subspecies *coloro*, is black with a broad yellow band. Rarely, a 'Desert' Black Swallowtail, form *clarki*, occurs that resembles the typical Black Swallowtail of much of the U.S. where the yellow band is much more restricted.

The 'Desert' Black has the upperside forewing marginal spots more rounded compared to the similar Anise Swallowtail (opposite) with more elongate spots. For positive identification of the 'Desert' Black, look closely or with binoculars for a row of tiny yellow dots on each side of the abdomen above a lateral yellow band (two bands for females).

Males sip mud and patrol on hilltops for females. Both sexes sip flowers—Chuparosa, Deerweed, Desert Apricot, Butterweed. They fly in desert transition habitats such as Plum Canyon, Sentenac Cienaga, Montezuma Vista Point.

Caterpillar Food Plant and Caterpillars

CITRUS FAMILY: Turpentine Broom, *Thamnosma montana* (below).

Turpentine Broom, an aromatic shrub 1'–3' tall, has chartreuse stems and small double fruits.

The small purple flowers of Turpentine Broom bloom from Feb to Jun.

'Desert' Black Swallowtail caterpillars on Turpentine Broom showing dark and white forms.

ANISE SWALLOWTAIL
Papilio zelicaon

Size: Large (2¼"–3")   *Flies:* Jan–Dec (several flights)

Anise Swallowtail sipping moist sand

Boulder Co. CO 7 May 1999

The Anise Swallowtail, common in most of California except in deserts, is black with a broad yellow band, difficult to distinguish from the 'Desert' Black Swallowtail (opposite). In general Anise flies in chaparral or in the mountains in our area. Both swallowtails may fly together where habitats overlap and the caterpillar food plants of both butterflies grow. To tell them apart, check the upperside marginal yellow spots, more elongate in Anise, more rounded in 'Desert' Black. To be positive you must look at the abdomen. The Anise has no tiny yellow dots above the yellow lateral band of the males (or two bands for females) on each side of the black abdomen, a feature visible up close or with binoculars. The 'Desert' Black does have dots.

Males avidly patrol hilltops awaiting females, now and then stopping to perch or to sip moist sand or mud. Both sexes nectar at many flowers. Look for the Anise at hilltops such as Kwaaymii Point, Garnet Peak, Combs Peak and Montezuma Vista Point.

Its caterpillars eat several native plants in the Carrot Family as listed below. In addition, the Anise caterpillars eat cultivated and exotic plants—anise, fennel, celery, Queen Anne's Lace. With the advent of citrus groves in California, its caterpillars now avidly eat citrus trees, since Citrus Family plants contain some essential oils very similar to Carrot Family plant oils.

Caterpillar Food Plants

CARROT FAMILY: Woolly-Fruit Lomatium, *Lomatium dasycarpum* (below); Southern Tauschia, *Tauschia arguta* (p. 20); Rattlesnake Weed, *Daucus pusillus,* & Pacific Oenanthe, *Oenanthe sarmentosa* (not shown).

Garnet Peak SD Co, CA 4 May 2000

Woolly-Fruit Lomatium, a perennial 12"–18" tall, has short stems, dissected leaves and whitish flowers in umbels in bloom Apr–Jun. It grows in rocky places.

Garnet Peak SD Co, CA 7 May 2001

Anise Swallowtail male perching on a hilltop shrub after patrolling for several minutes

19

INDRA SWALLOWTAIL
Papilio indra pergamus

Size: Medium–Large: (2"–2³/₄")   *Flies:* Feb–Jul (1 flight)

Garnet Peak SD Co, CA 27 Apr 2001

Indra Swallowtail perching on manzanita

The Indra Swallowtail is black. Our southern California subspecies *pergamus* has long tails. (Some subspecies have short to stubby tails.) Compared to the 'Desert' Black or Anise Swallowtail, Indra has a narrower and paler yellow band across the black wings, similar on both upper- and undersides. To verify you have an Indra, look at the abdomen. It will be black, with or without a short pale yellow stripe on each side near the posterior end.

Indra Swallowtail males both perch and patrol just below the peaks of our desert mountains. You may see these handsome shiny black swallowtails flying above the dense chaparral vegetation or perching on shrubs at locations such as Combs Peak, Kwaaymii Point and Garnet Peak. Or, look for them in locales such as Culp Valley or Lower Oriflamme Canyon where you may find a male sipping moisture from mud and damp sand or either sex sipping nectar from flowers such as Narrowleaf Goldenbush.

Another black swallowtail that occasionally may be sighted as a stray is the **Pipevine Swallowtail** (p. 104) with a blue-green iridescence and large orange spots on the underside.

Caterpillar Food Plants

CARROT FAMILY: Southern Tauschia, *Tauschia arguta* (below); Shiny Lomatium, *Lomatium lucidum* (not shown).

Garnet Peak SD Co, CA 20 May 1997

Southern Tauschia is a beautiful low perennial only 12"–30" high, with semi-glossy sharply-toothed pinnate leaves and flowers in yellow umbels. It grows in desert transition or chaparral, often along trails in the shade of tall shrubs, at Culp Valley, Combs Peak, Kwaaymii Point and Garnet Peak.

GIANT SWALLOWTAIL
Papilio cresphontes

Size: Large (3¹/₄"–5¹/₂")   *Flies:* Mar–Dec (several flights)

Giant Swallowtail sipping Lantana

Borrego Springs, CA 5 Sept 1990

The Giant Swallowtail is our largest butterfly! This swallowtail features a distinctive continuous horizontal yellow band across all wings and black spoon-shaped tails filled with yellow. Its abdomen is cream with a black stripe along the top.

Look for this "giant" swallowtail not in wild areas, but in the citrus groves of Borrego Springs and Borrego Valley and also in the residential areas where citrus trees are part of the home landscaping. In 1963 the Giant Swallowtail "invaded" the citrus groves of southern California. Its caterpillars, which feed on native plants in the Citrus Family in many other parts of the country, can readily eat the tender young shoots and leaves of citrus trees such as lemon, orange and grapefruit.

Giant Swallowtail males patrol for females. Adults sip mud or wet sand and are avid visitors to flowers. In Borrego Springs the favorite nectar sources for the Giant (and for several other butterflies as well) are Lantanas, common landscape shrubs with arching branches and clusters of gold-orange-red flowers or pink-yellow flowers. In our area Giant Swallowtails seem to be sporadic uncommon visitors. Yet twice in separate years, we saw a Giant stop in front of our home in Borrego Springs to sip nectar from our Lantana bushes. Special occasions!

Caterpillar Food Plants

CITRUS FAMILY: **Lemon,** *Citrus limon* (below); other *Citrus* species.

Borrego Springs, CA 22 Mar 2001

Lemon blossoms. Lemons and other citrus fruits, with their sweet white blossoms and glossy evergreen leaves are a familiar sight in Borrego Springs.

Santa Anna NWR, TX 31 May 1997

Giant Swallowtail showing the distinctive horizontal yellow band.

21

WESTERN TIGER SWALLOWTAIL
Papilio rutulus

Size: Large (2¹/₂"–3¹/₂")   *Flies:* Jan–Dec (several flights)

Hellhole Canyon ABDSP CA 14 Mar 2002

Western Tiger Swallowtail sipping Chuparosa nectar

One of the grandest butterflies in our area! Here these large yellow swallowtails with vertical black tiger stripes live in the moist canyons where their major caterpillar food plant, the California Sycamore, grows.

The yellow Western Tiger with black stripes is easy to tell apart from the similar Pale Swallowtail (opposite) that is cream with black stripes. However, the underside, seen when perched with wings closed, is less distinctive; the Tiger is more yellowish (see p. 7) while the Pale is whitish (see p. 17).

Western Tiger Swallowtails are very strong fliers. Males patrol up and down canyons and continue out the canyon washes, flying fast and high in the important search for females. Occasionally they come down to earth to visit flowers or to sip moisture from mud or sand or even, as happened to me, to sip sweat from a tee shirt!

Both male and female Western Tigers nectar on flowers such as Chuparosa and Yerba Santa. Look for these swallowtails in places such as Hellhole Canyon, Borrego Palm Canyon, Culp Valley and other riparian areas where California Sycamores grow.

Caterpillar Food Plants

SYCAMORE FAMILY: California Sycamore, *Plantanus racemosa* (below), in our area the main food plant. Also: BIRCH FAMILY: Mountain Alder, *Alnus rhombifolia* (not shown); WILLOW FAMILY: Slender Willow, *Salix exigua* (pp. 44, 82), Arroyo Willow, *S. lasiolepis* (not shown).

Hellhole Canyon ABDSP CA 7 Mar 2000

California Sycamores are tall trees which grow along canyon streams. Their bark separates and falls away, exposing distinctive whitish patches of the inner bark. Their large lobed leaves indicate this is a riparian plant. Several "balls" of fruit hang down on a single stalk.

PALE SWALLOWTAIL
Papilio eurymedon

Size: Large (2¹/₂"–3¹/₂")   *Flies:* Feb–Oct (2–3 flights)

Pale Swallowtail nectaring on Yerba Santa

Culp Valley ABDSP, CA 8 Apr 1996

The large Pale Swallowtail is readily distinguished from the similar Tiger (opposite) by its cream and black tiger stripes on the upperside. However, when perched with wings closed, Pales and Tigers look much alike on the underside; Pales are whiter (see p. 17) whereas Tigers are more yellowish (see p. 7).

Pale Swallowtails inhabit desert transition, chaparral and montane habitats where the several shrubs that serve as their caterpillar food plants grow. Pale Swallowtail males are strong fliers and are hilltoppers. At hilltops such as Garnet Peak, Stephenson Peak and Montezuma Vista Point, we see Pales, from a single male to a group of four or more, soaring and circling round and round in a frenzied flight above the peaks searching for females.

However, males often come down from the hilltops to sip wet sand and mud and nectar in riparian canyons such as Hellhole Canyon and Culp Valley where they can be approached and observed rather closely. Females also sip wet sand and both sexes nectar at Chuparosa, Yerba Santa and Manzanita.

Caterpillar Food Plants

BUCKTHORN FAMILY: Hoary Coffeeberry, *Rhamnus tomentella* (below left); Wedgeleaf Ceanothus, *Ceanothus cuneatus* (p. 45). ROSE FAMILY: Western Chokecherry, *Prunus virginiana* (below right); Hollyleaf Cherry, *P. ilicifolia* (not shown).

Upper Oriflamme Canyon ABDSP, CA 6 May 2000

Doane Pond Palomar Mountain SP, CA 29 May 2003

Hoary Coffeeberry is a shrub under 20' tall of chaparral and woodlands with leaves green above, whitish woolly beneath, small whitish flowers May–Jul and red berries.

Western Chokecherry, a shrub to small tree 3'–18' tall of rocky slopes, has deciduous ovate leaves, small white flowers in a cylindrical cluster Apr–Jun and dark red berries.

23

Whites & Sulphurs (PIERIDAE)

These are white, yellow or orange butterflies, often marked with black. Male and female may differ in appearance (sexual dimorphism). Species with two or more broods per year often have distinctive seasonal variations. Spring flights have the underside of the wing darker scaled than the summer flight. And in more tropical areas, the winter (dry) flight is darker than the summer (wet) flight. There are about 60 species in the U.S. with 19 species recorded in our area.

TWO SUBFAMILIES occur in Anza-Borrego Desert State Park® and environs.

WHITES (PIERINAE) including Whites, Marbles and Orangetips are mainly white with black markings. Orangetips, which have an orangish patch on their forewings tips, and Marbles have a greenish mosslike marbling pattern on their underside hindwings. (8 species)

SULPHURS (COLIADINAE), like the chemical sulphur, are yellow or orange-yellow, often with black borders on the upperside of the wings. They usually sit with wings closed. The word *butterfly* may have been derived from an European yellow species. (11 species)

| *Spring White* | *California Marble* | *Sara Orangetip* | *Harford's Sulphur* |
| A **WHITE** | A **WHITE** | A **WHITE** | A **SULPHUR** |

HABITS:
- All feed on floral nectar and sip damp sand or mud, often in groups.
- Flight is generally straight, steady and fluttering. Some strong fliers undertake long distance mass migrations for reasons unknown.
- Males patrol to search for females.

PLANTS EATEN BY THE CATERPILLARS: In our area, **WHITES** eat plants in the Mustard Family or the closely related Caper Family, both containing mustard oils making Whites distasteful to vertebrate predators. **SULPHURS** eat plants in the Pea Family, except for the Dainty Sulphur, which eats plants in the Sunflower Family.

Eggs: Pierid eggs are long, spindle-shaped, usually pale hues that later change to orange/red. Most are laid singly on leaves, stems, buds or flowers of the food plant, but a few species lay eggs in clusters.

Caterpillar (larva): Caterpillars are cylindrical, rather smooth and covered with short, fine hairs (setae) that are often clumped into low tubercles. Young caterpillars of both subfamilies have forked hairs on the body that dispense honeydew from their tips to attract ants in exchange for protection.

Chrysalis (pupa): Chrysalises, attached by both a silk pad and a silk girdle around the middle, are cryptic, resembling buds, new leaves, flowers, or even bird droppings.

Hibernation: In temperate regions most **WHITES** overwinter as chrysalises, most **SULPHURS** as caterpillars. The more tropical species hibernate as adults and then migrate northward during the spring and summer to recolonize.

BECKER'S WHITE
Pontia beckerii

Size: Medium (1⅝"–2")　　　　　　　　　*Flies:* Jan–Dec (2–3 flights)

Becker's White perching on Buckwheat

Sentenac Canyon ABDSP, CA 14 Mar 1997

Becker's White is a butterfly of desert and desert transition. It has a prominent squarish black forewing spot often centered with white. On the underside the yellow hind-wing veins have wide olive green borders, heavier in the spring than in the summer, interrupted at about the middle of the wing by an open white area. The sexes are dimorphic with females more heavily marked on the upperside.

Males patrol Borrego Valley desert washes, Hellhole, Borrego Palm and Plum Canyons, Yaqui Well, wherever Bladderpod grows.

Becker's White nectars at many flowers including Spanish Needles, Bladderpod, Desert Lavender and Buckwheat.

Yaqui Well ABDSP, CA 26 Feb 1999

Becker's White male on Bladderpod

Yaqui Well ABDSP, CA 10 Mar 2000

Becker's White female, more heavily marked than male, sipping Bladderpod

The Caterpillar Food Plant, Caterpillar and Chrysalis

CAPER FAMILY: Bladderpod, *Isomeris arborea* (below left, center, right).

Hellhole Canyon ABDSP, CA 18 Mar 2003

Sentenac Canyon ABDSP, CA 14 Mar 1997

Sentenac Canyon ABDSP, CA 22 Mar 1997

Bladderpod, a rounded shrub 3'–5' tall of washes and canyons, has a pungent odor. Yellow flowers may bloom any month, followed by inflated seed pods.

Becker's White caterpillar on Bladderpod

Becker's White chrysalis on Bladderpod

SPRING WHITE
Pontia sisymbrii

Size: Small–Medium (1¼"–1¾")   *Flies:* Feb–Jun (1 flight)

San Felipe Valley-BLM SD Co, CA 18 Mar 1999

Spring White nectaring on Filaree

The delicate Spring White, a very early spring butterfly in our area, flies in many different habitats.

The sexes are dimorphic. The forewings of both sexes have black markings, with the male's markings lighter, the female's heavier and more extensive. On the underside hindwings the gray or tannish veins edged with blackish-brown are slightly interrupted past midwing by a white area.

Males patrol hilltops or along canyon bottoms awaiting females. Adults nectar at flowers, including Desert Apricot, Desert Pincushion and Filaree. Look for this butterfly in Plum, Hellhole and Oriflamme Canyons, Sentenac Cienega and Scissors Crossing/San Felipe Valley and Borrego Springs.

San Felipe Valley ABDSP, CA 11 Mar 2000

Spring White male sipping mud

Hellhole Canyon ABDSP, CA 18 Mar 2003

Spring White female sipping Desert Pincushion

Caterpillar Food Plants, Egg and Caterpillar

MUSTARD FAMILY: Many including: Payson's Jewelflower, *Caulanthus simulans* (below left & center & p. 31); Nevada Rockcress, *Arabis perennans* (below right & p. 29); Sicklepod Rockcress, *A. sparsiflora* (p. 29); California Mustard, *Guillenia lasiophylla* (p. 28); Tumble Mustard, *Sisymbrium altissimum* & Jewelflowers, *Streptanthus spp.* (not shown).

San Felipe Valley-BLM SD Co, CA 20 Mar 2003

San Felipe Val, CA 26 Apr 2001

Caterpillar eating pods of Payson's Jewelflower

Left: ***Payson's Jewelflower***, an annual 12"–21" tall, has "eared" stem leaves, yellow flowers Mar–May.

Banner SD Co, CA 12 Mar 2002

Egg on Nevada Rockcress, a perennial of rocky slopes with purple to pink flowers Mar–May and recurved seed pods.

CHECKERED WHITE
Pontia protodice

Size: Small–Medium (1¹/₂"–2")   *Flies:* Jan–Dec (sev flights)

Checkered White nectaring on Golden Yarrow

Jacumba ABDSP, CA 25 Apr 2001

Checkered Whites are among the most versatile butterflies in our area. They fly in every habitat from the low desert to montane, possibly because the many mustards the caterpillars eat grow almost everywhere.

Checkered Whites are dimorphic with females more heavily marked than males. The underside hindwing is variable. Veins may be edged with brown, yellow-brown, or even greenish, often appearing smudgy. Some summer males have pure white underside hindwings.

Males patrol for females on hilltops and near food plants. Nectar plants include Spanish Needles, Fiddleneck, Desert Lavender, Desert Arrowweed, Buckwheat, Alkali Goldenbush and Sandpaper Plant.

Borrego Sink Borrego Springs, CA 3 May 2001

Borrego Springs, CA 7 May 2001

Checkered White male sipping Desert Arrowweed

Female newly emerged from her chrysalis

Caterpillar Food Plants and Chrysalis

MUSTARD FAMILY: many including: Tansy Mustard, *Descurainia pinnata* (below left & p. 30); Turnip Mustard, *Brassica tournefortii* (below center & right); Tumble Mustard, *Sisymbrium altissimum* (not shown).

Bitter Creek Canyon ABDSP, CA 9 Mar 2003

Flat Cat Canyon ABDSP, CA 16 Mar 2001

Borrego Springs, CA 3 May 2001

Tansy Mustard, an annual mustard 4"–24" tall, has dissected lacy leaves, yellow flowers Mar-Jun and club-like seed pods.

Turnip Mustard, a weedy annual mustard 4"–24" tall, has pinnified leaves and pale yellow flowers.

Checkered White chrysalis on Turnip Mustard.

27

CABBAGE WHITE
Pieris rapae
Size: Med (1⅝"–2")   *Flies:* Jan–Dec (sev flts)

Cabbage White female on Wild Heliotrope

The Cabbage White introduced from Europe, though most common in towns and orchards, may occur almost anywhere. We have seen it near the citrus groves in Borrego Springs, in Sentenac Cienega, and on Garnet Peak. Males patrol around mustards looking for females. Adults nectar on Wild Heliotrope and many other flowers.

On the upperside the forewing tip is gray. Males have one black dot on the forewing, females have two. The underside wings are creamy with gray forewing tips.

Caterpillar Food Plants

MUSTARD FAMILY: many including London Rocket, *Sisymbrium irio* (below); Tumble Mustard, *S. altissimum* & Cooper's Caulanthus, *Caulanthus cooperi* (not shown).

London Rocket is a weedy annual mustard 8"–32" tall with small yellow flowers that bloom Jan–Apr and ascending seed pods. It grows in Borrego Valley, Sentenac Cienega.

CALIFORNIA MARBLE
Euchloe hyantis
Size: Small (1¼"–1½")   *Flies:* Mar–Jul (1 flt)

California Marble on Cupleaf Ceanothus

The California Marble, our one true Marble, is whitish on the upper side with a black forewing bar and black checked wing tips. The white underside hindwing is heavily marbled with greenish-yellow bands.

Look for the California Marble wherever its native mustard caterpillar food plants grow, places such as the Scissors Crossing area, Sentenac Canyon, Jacumba, and Garnet Peak. Males patrol hilltops such as Garnet Peak and sometimes around the food plants awaiting females.

Caterpillar and its Food Plants

MUSTARD FAM: including California Mustard, *Guillenia lasiophylla* (below); Tansy Mustard, *Descurainia pinnata* (pp. 27, 30); Jewelflowers, *Streptanthus* spp (not shown).

California Marble caterpillar eating seed pods of California Mustard, an annual 4"–24" tall with whitish blooms Mar-Jun. Cylindrical seed pods abruptly bend downward.

'GRINNELL'S' GRAY MARBLE
Anthocharis lanceolata australis
Size: Med (1½"–1⅞")   *Flies:* Mar–May (1 flt)

'Grinnell's' Marble on Sicklepod Rockcress

The Gray Marble, unique with its pointed white forewing and gray or brown striated underside hindwing, is not a Marble but an Orangetip without orange patches.

Gray Marble males patrol along canyons bottoms or cliffsides for females, rarely resting or sipping flowers and so, it's hard to know for sure if you are seeing this butterfly!

This subspecies *australis* flies at higher elevations where its caterpillars eat Sicklepod Rockcress. Look for it at Kwaaymii Point, San Felipe Hills or near Combs Peak.

Caterpillar Food Plant

MUSTARD FAMILY: Sicklepod Rockcress, *Arabis sparsiflora* (above & below).

Sicklepod Rockcress, a perennial 12"–30" tall with pink to purple flowers Apr–May and seed pods like sickles, grows in dry stony places such as rocky slopes or cliffs.

'DESERT EDGE' GRAY MARBLE
Anthocharis lanceolata desertolimbus
Size: Sm-Med (1¼"–1⅝")   *Flies:* Feb–Apr (1 flt)

'Desert Edge' Gray Marble
Above: *on grass*
Right: *sipping Mulefat*

This newly-described subspecies *deserto-limbus* ('desert edge') flies in transition areas such as Culp Valley and Scissors Crossing where its caterpillars eat Nevada Rockcress. Easiest to tell from *australis* (left) by habitat and food plant, it has more dark scaling on the underside.

Caterpillar Food Plant

MUSTARD FAMILY: Nevada Rockcress, *Arabis perennans* (below & p. 26).

Nevada Rockcress, a perennial 8"–24" tall of rocky slopes, canyon walls and pinyon-juniper woodlands, has purple to pinkish flowers Mar–May and recurved seed pods.

29

DESERT ORANGETIP
Anthocharis cethura

Size: Small (1¹/₈"–1¹/₂")　　　　　　　　　　　*Flies:* Jan–Jun (1 flight)

Desert Orangetip male nectaring on Fiddleneck

The Desert Orangetip, a true desert dweller, sensibly flies only in the springtime in the arid southwestern U.S.

Its orangish patches (variable from bright to very pale) on white forewings are shared only with Sara Orangetip (opposite page) in our area, but the Desert has white indentations on the wingtip margin lacking in Sara. Females have white intermixed with black above the orange patch. On the underside the heavy green marbling is fused into bands, more so than for Sara.

Look for Desert Orangetips hilltopping at Montezuma Vista Point, Scissors Crossing/ San Felipe Valley and Plum and Bitter Creek Canyons. They sip many spring flowers such as Fiddleneck, Desert Apricot, Filaree and Evening Primroses.

Desert Orangetip female with a very pale orange patch

Desert Orangetips, mating pair

Caterpillar Food Plants and Caterpillars

MUSTARD FAMILY: Lacepod, *Thysanocarpus curvipes* (below left & center);Tansy Mustard, *Descurainia pinnata* (below right & p. 27); Payson's Jewelflower, *Caulanthus simulans* (pp. 26, 31); Cooper's Caulanthus, *C. cooperi* & Longbeak Twistflower, *Streptanthella longirostris* (not shown).

Lacepod, an annual 12"–18" tall, has basal leaves, "eared" stem leaves, tiny white to purplish flowers Mar–May and distinctive seed pods.

Desert Orangetip caterpillar on Lacepod eating a winged roundish seed pod.

Desert Orangetip caterpillar on Tansy Mustard, eating an ascending club-shaped seed pod.

30

SARA ORANGETIP
Anthocharis sara (= thoosa)

Size: Small (1"–1¹/₂")   *Flies:* Feb–Jun (1-2 flights)

Sara Orangetip male nectaring on Desert Apricot

Watching the male Sara Orangetip busily patrol up and down desert canyons is one of the joys of early spring. With white wings tipped orange (brighter in males) and edged with black, they are small but conspicuous. Females have a white band between the orange patch and black. Some females are yellowish. The underside has patches of dark mossy marbling.

In our area only Sara and the similar Desert Orangetip (opposite page) have orange wingtips. Sara males patrol for females along gulches and canyons; Desert males hilltop.

This spring butterfly flies almost everywhere. It sips many flowers—Desert Lavender, Desert Lotus, Desert Pincushion, Spanish Needles, Bladderpod, Fernleaf Phacelia, Desert Apricot.

Sara female with white band between orange patch and black wing edge sipping Chia

Sara Orangetips, mating pair with female below

Caterpillar Food Plants, Egg and Caterpillar

MUSTARD FAMILY: Hall's Caulanthus, *Caulanthus hallii* (below left & center); Payson's Jewelweed, *C. simulans* (below right & p. 26); Nevada Rockcress, *Arabis perennans* (pp. 26, 29); Turnip Mustard, *Brassica tournefortii* (p. 27); Tansy Mustard, *Descurainia pinnata* (pp. 27, 30); Lacepod, *Thysanocarpus curvipes* (p. 30).

Hall's Caulanthus, an annual 8"– 36" tall, has "earless" stem leaves and yellowish blooms on long pedicels (flower stalks) Mar–May.

Sara Egg on Hall's Caulanthus

Hall's Caulanthus flowers

Sara caterpillar on Payson's Jewelweed. Its flowers have short hairy pedicels (flower stalks).

31

ORANGE SULPHUR
Colias eurytheme

Size: Medium (1³/₈"–2¹/₄")   *Flies:* Jan–Dec (several flights)

Culp Valley, ABDSP, CA 18 Oct 2003

Orange Sulphur male. Note the upperside black border seen faintly through the wing

The Orange Sulphur comes in shades of orange, yellow and white with black markings. Both sexes, except for an occasional white female, show some charactertistic orange coloration on the upperside as seen when flying since they sit with wings closed.

The sexes are dimorphic with male uppersides having solid black borders while females have borders with interrupted light areas giving a ladder effect.

Males patrol looking for females. Adults sip moist sand and nectar at many flowers.

Orange Sulphurs are found throughout the U.S. with multiple broods. We see them fly from Borrego Valley to Culp Valley to Garnet Peak Trail, more commonly in fall.

The very similar **Clouded Sulphur** (p. 105), a rare stray here, and the Hartford's Sulphur (opposite) have no upperside orange.

Boulder Co, CO 1 Oct 2000

Orange Sulphur white female. Most females are yellow/orange.

Caterpillar Food Plants

PEA FAMILY: many including the following natives: Desert Rattlepod, *Astragalus crotalariae* (left); Bishop Lotus, *Lotus strigosus* (below); Deerweed, *Lotus scoparius* (pp. 48, 57, 59); Miniature Lupine, *Lupinus bicolor* (p. 59).

Wind Caves Split Mt ABDSP, CA 27 Mar 1994

Culp Valley ABDSP, CA 20 Mar 2001

Desert Rattlepod, an erect annual or perennial 6"–24" high of sandy deserts, has wands of reddish-purple flowers Jan–Apr and inflated pods.

Bishop Lotus, a prostrate annual, often with fleshy leaves, has bright yellow pea-like flowers Feb–Jun that turn reddish after pollination. It grows in many habitats from deserts to montane meadows.

HARFORD'S SULPHUR
Colias harfordii (=*C. alexandra harfordii*)

Size: Medium (1³/₄"–2")   *Flies:* Feb–Nov or possibly all year (2-3 flights)

Harford's Sulphur male, spring form with dark scaling, sipping Mulefat. The upperside narrow black border is faintly visible.

Culp Valley ABDSP, CA 21 Mar 1996

Harford's Sulphur is the common yellow butterfly in our region. It never displays orange as does the Orange Sulphur. Harford's flies in many habitats from desert bajadas and canyons to chaparral and montane, wherever the Locoweeds its caterpillars eat grow. Adults are sexually dimorphic and also have seasonal forms. Males are brighter yellow and have strong though narrow black borders; female borders are more diffuse. Some spring adults in our area have black scaling on the underside hindwings, while summer adults are clearer yellow. Females have no white form.

Males patrol back and forth, cruising rapidly and stopping infrequently. Adults sip moist sand and mud and nectar at many flowers including Sweetbush, Sawtooth Goldenbush, Fernleaf Phacelia, Wild Onion and the caterpillar food plant Parish Locoweed.

Garnet Peak SD Co, CA 20 May 1997

Harford's Sulphur male, the bright yellow summer form, nectaring on Wild Onion

Caterpillar Food Plants

PEA FAMILY: Parish Locoweed, *Astragalus douglasii* var *parishii* (below); Palmer Locoweed, *A. palmeri* (p. 53); sometimes Deerweed, *Lotus scoparius* (pp. 48, 57, 59).

Cuyamaca Rancho St Pk SD Co, CA 24 Jun 2000

Parish Locoweed, a mat-like perennial 16"–40" across of woods and open slopes, has pinnate leaves, whitish to yellow pea-like flowers Apr–Aug and strongly inflated seed pods.

Garnet Peak SD Co, CA 20 May 1997

Harford's Sulphur female on Southern Tauschia leaves

CALIFORNIA DOGFACE
Zerene (= *Colias*) *eurydice*

Size: Medium (2"–2³/₈")   *Flies:* Jan–Dec; usually Mar–Sep (2 flights)

*California Dogface male
perched on Desert Scrub Oak*

The spectacular California Dogface is California's State Butterfly. Male upperside forewings show a golden poodle "face" and "eye" overlaid with a purplish sheen against a black border. Sulphurs sit with wings closed, so look for this "face" when males are flying or wings are backlighted. Pure yellow females have one black spot on each forewing.

We see this striking butterfly along canyon streams at Hellhole/Culp Valley, Borrego Palm and Lower Oriflamme Canyons.

Males patrol for females, usually near food plants. Adults sip moist sand and flowers.

Similar but uncommon species are the **Southern Dogface** with no purplish sheen (p. 105) and the **Mexican Yellow** and **Boisduval's Yellow** (both p. 105) with vague "faces" and no "eyes".

Backlighted male showing the poodle "face"

Female underside. Her pale yellow upperside has no poodle "face"

Male upperside

Caterpillar Food Plant, Egg, Caterpillar

PEA FAMILY: False Indigo, *Amorpha fruticosa* (below left and right & p. 88).

Egg on False Indigo

Left: *California Dogface caterpillar on False Indigo*

False Indigo, a deciduous shrub 3'–6' tall with pinnate leaves and small flowers with a dark purple banner arranged in a long spike, grows along streams in canyons.

DAINTY SULPHUR
Nathalis iole

Size: Tiny–Small (³/₄"–1¹/₈") *Flies:* Feb–Dec (several flights)

Dainty Sulphur
Near right: *summer form at Snakeweed*
Far right: *winter form*

Culp Valley, ABDSP, CA 18 Oct 2003

Hellhole Canyon, ABDSP, CA 3 Mar 1998

Dainty Sulphurs are the smallest sulphurs in the U.S. Underside hindwings have darker scaling in the winter form, lighter in the summer form. On the upper-side males are pale yellow; females, dull orangish yellow; black markings, more extensive in females, include a band at the forewing's lower edge.

Dainty Sulphurs start flying by mid February along roadsides in Borrego Springs and in sandy canyons such as Hellhole, Plum, Box. Later they may show up almost anywhere. Males patrol inches above the ground or perch on gravel or sand for females. Adults sip composites. Unlike our other sulphurs the caterpillars eat plants in the Sunflower family.

The somewhat similar small **Mimosa Yellow** (p. 105) is a rare stray.

Borrego Springs, CA 19 Feb 2000

Dainty Sulphurs, winter form, mating pair

Caterpillar Food Plants

SUNFLOWER FAMILY: Spanish Needles, *Palafoxia arida* (below left); Cinchweed, *Pectis papposa* (below center); San Felipe Dyssodia, *Adenophyllum porophylloides* (below right).

Borrego Springs, CA 5 Mar 2001; *Insert:* 19 Feb 2000

Borrego Palm Canyon ABDSP, CA 11 Oct 2003

Upper Tubb Can. ABDSP, CA 18 Oct '03; *Insert:* 2 May '01

Spanish Needles, an annual 4"–28" tall of sandy deserts, has pink disk flowers with purplish anthers Oct–Apr.

Cinchweed, a scented annual mounded to 8" tall, has small yellow flowers and phyllaries with glands Jun and Sep-Dec.

San Felipe Dyssodia, an odor-ous subshrub 8"–24" tall, has yellow/red flowers with gland-dotted phyllaries Oct–May.

35

SLEEPY ORANGE
Eurema (= *Abaeis*) *nicippe*

Size: Medium (1¹/₂"–2") *Flies:* Jan–Dec (several flights)

Box Canyon ABDSP, CA 23 Feb 1998

Sleepy Orange, winter/dry season form, nectaring on Desert Lotus

Sleepy Orange with its unique yellowish-orange wings with black borders on the upperside is easy to spot on wing even though it flies rapidly and erratically, anything but sleepily! The curved black line on the upper forewing, some think, resembles a closed eye, hence its common name. It always perches with wings closed. The underside has two forms, a brownish winter/dry season form similar to a dried leaf or a bright yellow summer/wet season form.

Adults sip wet sand or mud and nectar at flowers such as Deerweed and Desert Lotus. Males patrol desert and desert transition sandy canyons and washes such as Borrego Palm, Bitter Creek, Plum and Box Canyons, Senna Wash, Culp Valley.

Borrego Sink Borrego Springs, CA 17 Oct 2003

Borrego Springs, CA Jun 1991

Sleepy Orange, summer form, sipping Jackass Clover

Sleepy Orange upperside (roadkill)

Caterpillar Food Plants, Egg and Caterpillar

PEA FAMILY: Coues' Cassia, *Senna covesii* (below left); Desert Cassia, *S. armata* (below right & p. 37).

Bitter Creek Canyon ABDSP, CA 28 Apr 2001

Senna Wash ABDSP, CA 7 May 2001

Coues' Cassia is a low bush 1'–2' high with three pair of leaflets. Each flower raceme has a few bright yellow flowers which bloom Apr–Jun. It grows in dry washes.

Sleepy Orange caterpillar eating Desert Cassia, described on opposite page. Insert: ***Egg on Desert Cassia.***

CLOUDLESS SULPHUR
Phoebis sennae

Size: Medium–Large (2"–2³/₄") *Flies:* Jan–Dec (usually Mar–May in deserts)

Cloudless Sulphur male

Cloudless Sulphurs are our largest sulphur. They are strong fliers, flying high overhead. These tropical butterflies migrate into our area and may become temporary residents in years of adequate rainfall.

Undersides vary from a warm yellow to a pale greenish yellow with males more lightly marked than females; in the center of the hindwing are two pink-rimmed silver spots. On the upperside males are an unmarked bright yellow, while females may be either yellow or white with a black spot and an irregular black edging around the margins.

Males patrol desert and desert transition washes and canyons such as Hellhole and Plum Canyons and Senna Wash. Adults sip mud or wet sand and nectar at flowers including Chuparosa and Brittlebush. Look for it in residential areas, too, where a nectar favorite, Bougainvillea, grows.

Cloudless Sulphur female on Brittlebush, golden in the warm light near sunset

Caterpillar Food Plants and Caterpillar

PEA FAMILY: Desert Cassia, *Senna armata* (below & p. 36); Coues' Cassia, *S. covesii* (p. 36).

Cloudless Sulphur on Desert Cassia, a shrub 2'–6' tall of sandy desert washes with erect green almost leafless branches from the base.

Cloudless Sulphur caterpillar eating Desert Cassia.

Desert Cassia in bloom. Long terminal inflorescences of showy golden flowers bloom Mar-May followed by long narrow pods.

37

Coppers, Hairstreaks & Blues (LYCAENIDAE)

This is a large, diverse family of small butterflies often called Gossamer-wings because they are dainty and delicate. They come in shades of brown, orange, gray, green and blue. Some display a metallic sheen of brilliant copper, purple, green or blue arising from the microscopic structure of the wing scales rather than pigmentation. Males and females of the same species often differ in color and pattern on the upperwing surfaces, although similar on the underwings. Males, with the front two legs somewhat reduced in length, rely upon the other four legs for walking. Of the 122 species found in the U.S., 39 species may be found in our area.

THREE SUBFAMILIES occur in Anza-Borrego Desert State Park® and environs.

COPPERS (LYCAENINAE): Named for the metallic coppery upper surface of males found in some species. (4 species)

HAIRSTREAKS (THECLINAE): Named for the tiny hair-like hindwing tails and fine, hair-like lines or streaks crossing the underside hindwing of many species. Some species, including our common Bramble Hairstreak and Brown Elfin, lack both tails and streaks. (17 species)

BLUES (POLYOMMATINAE): Named for the metallic blue upper surface of males. (18 species)

Tailed Copper
A COPPER

Bramble Hairstreak
A HAIRSTREAK

Acmon Blue
A BLUE

HABITS:
* Almost all feed at floral nectar.
* Only the male Blues take moisture at wet sand or mud with any regularity.
* When sitting, they often perform "hindwing rubbing" with wings closed. It is thought the eyespots and antenna-like tails draw predators away from the face.
* Males both perch and patrol (patrolling mainly restricted to Blues) to locate mates.

PLANTS EATEN BY THE CATERPILLARS: A variety of plants from many dicotyledon families and one gymnosperm family are eaten. Caterpillars often eat fruits and flowers rather than leaves.

Eggs: Flattened and scuptured, shaped like sea urchins or turbins.

Caterpillar (larva): Typically slug-like, greenish, brownish or cream, and covered with fine soft hairs. In these Gossamer-Wings (and Metalmarks), ants "milk" caterpillars by rubbing a special gland with their antennae to stimulate the release of a tiny drip of sweet liquid called honeydew. In return ants protect the caterpillars from insect predators.

Chrysalis (pupa): Mainly oval in shape and rounded at both ends. The chrysalis may be attached by a fine silken girdle. Some species pupate underground or in litter at the base of the food plant.

Hibernation: Depending on species, as egg or chrysalis, rarely as partially grown caterpillar.

TAILED COPPER
Lycaena arota

Size: Small (1¹/₈"–1³/₈")   *Flies:* May–Sep (1 flight)

Tailed Copper perching on Sugarbush

The Tailed Copper, our only copper with a well-defined tail, is fairly uncommon in San Diego County. It lives in scattered colonies, including a small colony in Culp Valley where Oak Gooseberry, its caterpillar foot plant, grows in abundance.

Males are a coppery-brown on the upper surface, while females are orange with brown margins and markings.

Males perch to await females, usually on or very near the Oak Gooseberry. Adults avidly suck mud and flower nectar, including a favorite, Buckwheat.

Tailed Copper female on Oak Gooseberry. Tailed Copper males are coppery-brown on the upperside.

Culp Valley ABDSP, CA 16 May 1997

Caterpillar Food Plant

GOOSEBERRY FAMILY: Oak Gooseberry, *Ribes quercetorum* (below).

Oak Gooseberry, a deciduous shrub 2'–5' tall with leaves cleft into 3–5 toothed lobes and one spine at each leaf node, grows in desert transition and chaparral.

Oak Gooseberry flowers are small but conspicuous. Yellow tube flowers in groups of two to three grow on short peduncles Mar–Apr followed by round black berries.

39

GORGON COPPER
Lycaena gorgon
Size: Small (1¼"–1½")   *Flies:* Mar–Jul (1 flight)

Culp Valley ABDSP, CA 15 May 1997

Gorgon Copper on Tall Buckwheat

The Gorgon Copper resembles a large Blue with its pale gray underside and its row of orange spots. The male upperside is coppery brown, the female, grayish with yellow spots.

Adults nectar on Buckwheat flowers. Look for this copper in places such as Culp Valley where the caterpillar food plant, Tall Buckwheat, grows. Males both patrol and perch near Tall Buckwheat, which in the spring consists of basal leaves and tall stems. Caterpillars eat leaves.

Caterpillar Food Plant

BUCKWHEAT FAMILY: Tall Buckwheat, *Eriogonum elongatum* (below).

Culp Valley ABDSP, CA 18 Oct 2003

Tall Buckwheat is a 2'–6' tall perennial of rocky dry places with wavy basal leaves. Wands of small whitish to pinkish flower clusters bloom Aug–Nov.

GREAT COPPER
Lycaena xanthoides
Size: Sm–Med (1¼"–1¾")   *Flies:* May–Aug (1 flt)

Palomar Mountain SP, CA 27 Jun 2000

Great Copper male perched on Thistle

Great Coppers, our largest coppers, have a short tail-like stub. Gray undersides have black dots and a short orange zig-zag near the hindwing margin. Male uppersides are gray; females have black and orange markings.

Adults sip flowers—Cryptantha, Buckwheat, Thistle. Males perch to await females. This rather local copper flies in moist places at higher elevations where the caterpillars eat Willow Dock. Look for it along Banner Grade and Sunshine Highway and at Laguna Meadows.

Caterpillar Food Plants

BUCKWHEAT FAMILY: Willow Dock, *Rumex salicifolius* (below & p. 41); Curly Dock, *R. crispus* (not shown).

Laguna Meadows SD Co, CA 26 Jun 2000

Great Copper female investigating Willow Dock, a prostrate to erect perennial with stems 1'–3' high and leaves, sometimes wavy-edged, up to 8" long on long petioles.

PURPLISH COPPER
Lycaena helloides

Size: Small (1"–1³/₈")   *Flies:* Mar–Nov (several flights)

Purplish Copper male, underside

The sexes of the Purple Copper are dimorphic, differing in color and markings, but both have the orange zigzag band on the underside hindwing.

The coppery brown upper surface of the male with a brilliant metallic blue-purple reflection is an example of structural color. This blue-purple sheen is caused by the complex microscopic architecture of the wing scales that interact with light to give this striking color. (Page 11 discusses wing color.)

Adults visit flowers for nectar. The males perch in gullies and sometimes patrol short distances all day long to seek females.

Purplish Coppers are fond of moist mountain meadows where Willow Dock, a caterpillar food plant, grows. Some places to look for this species are at the Laguna Meadows and in the marshes near the shore of Cuyamaca Lake.

Caterpillar Food Plants

BUCKWHEAT FAMILY: Willow Dock, *Rumex salicifolius* (below & p. 40); Curly Dock, *R. crispus* (not shown).

Willow Dock, a plant of moist places such as the marshy west side of Lake Cuyamaca, has open long flower clusters May–Sep followed by shiny white seeds.

Above: Purplish Copper male, upperside, perching in a wet meadow. Notice the display of the beautiful purple structural color on the upperside forewing.

Purplish Copper female. Females are quite variable on the upperside, ranging from orangish to orange-brown to brown with no orange.

41

GREAT PURPLE HAIRSTREAK
Atlides halesus

Size: Medium (1¼"–1¾")   *Flies:* Feb–Nov (several flights)

San Felipe/ Scissors Crossing ABDSP, CA 6 Mar 2003

Sentenac Canyon ABDSP 9 Oct 1998

Great Purple Hairstreak, a male with a metallic aqua patch on its forewing, on California Juniper

Our largest hairstreak, the Great Purple Hairstreak, and our handsomest! Notice its two pair of fancy tails. It perches with wings together. But when it takes off and lands, the upper wings flash a brilliant blue.

Adults sip Buckwheat, Desert Arrowweed, Alkali Goldenbush.

Males like to perch high to await females—near the tops of mistletoe-laden mesquites at the Borrego Sink or atop Sugarbush, Desert Scrub Oak or California Juniper on hilltops. You may see two males circling each other above a shrub, each apparently trying to drive away its rival.

Great Purple Hairstreak female captured by a crab spider on Alkali Goldenbush. She lacks the aqua patch on her forewing.

Caterpillar Food Plants

MISTLETOE FAM: Desert Mistletoe, *Phoradendron californicum,* parasitic on Mesquites, Catclaw, Ironwood, Creosote (below left, center); Big Leaf Mistletoe, *P. macrophyllum,* on Sycamore, Cottonwoods, Willows (below right); Dense Mistletoe, *P. densum*, on California Juniper (not shown).

Yaqui Well ABDSP, CA 10 Mar 2000

Bitter Creek Canyon ABDSP, CA 13 Mar 2001

Oriflamme Canyon ABDSP, CA 13 Mar 2003

Great Purple male on Desert Mistletoe. It has scalelike leaves, flowers Dec–Mar and coral berries.

Desert Mistletoe, very evident when fruiting. Caterpillars eat male flowers, leaves and stems, not fruit.

Big Leaf Mistletoe on California Sycamore. It has largish leaves to 2" long, flowers Dec–Mar, whitish berries.

GOLDEN HAIRSTREAK
Habrodais grunus
Size: Small (1"–1¹/₄")   *Flies:* May–Sep (1 flight)

Golden Hairstreak on Canyon Live Oak leaf

The Golden Hairstreak is named for its golden underside. Notice its tail, typical of many hairstreaks. A row of light blue crescent spots forms a submarginal band.

Males tend to perch on the tips of sunlit branches of Canyon Live Oaks. They also patrol around treetops, especially late afternoons. Although adult Golden Hairstreaks do sip mud, they do not sip flower nectar. Look for them where Canyon Live Oaks grow in canyons and on slopes. We have seen them fly at Kwaaymii Point.

Caterpillar Food Plant

OAK FAMILY: Canyon Live Oak, *Quercus chrysolepis* (below & p. 83).

Golden Hairstreak perching on Canyon Live Oak, an evergreen shrub (var *nana,* above) or tree 20'–60' tall found on canyons or slopes with leaves entire or toothed with small spines.

GOLD-HUNTER'S HAIRSTREAK
Satyrium auretorum
Size: Small (1"–1¹/₄")   *Flies:* Apr–Aug (1 flight)

Gold–Hunter's Hairstreak

This butterfly, discovered during the California Gold Rush, was named for the gold hunters. Like gold, it is not common! We have not yet seen it. Males have very short tails, females (above) have longer tails. Near the tail is a small orange spot with a black center.

This is a butterfly of chaparral and oak woodlands where its caterpillars eat the new growth of scrub oaks. Males may patrol or perch on hilltops for females. Adults nectar on flowers such as buckwheat.

Caterpillar Food Plants

OAK FAMILY: Scrub Live Oak, *Quercus wislizeni* var *frutescens* (below); Canyon Live Oak, *Q. chrysolepis* (left & p. 83); Desert Scrub Oak, *Q. cornelius-mulleri* (p. 88).

Scrub Live Oak, an evergreen shrub 6'–18' tall, has shiny dark green leaves, paler below, either spiny-toothed or entire. It grows in chaparral, especially near Sunrise Hwy.

HEDGEROW HAIRSTREAK
Satyrium saepium
Size: Small (1"-1¹/₄") *Flies:* Apr–Aug (1 flight)

Hedgerow Hairstreak, the commonest chaparral hairstreak, perched on Sugarbush

The Hedgerow Hairstreak has a pale blue tailspot on the brownish to gray underside. The upperside, seen when flying, flashes a diagnostic coppery brown. Male tails are short; female tails are longer.

Males, avid hilltoppers, perch on the sides of chaparral shrubs to wait for females. Adults frequent flowers such as Buckwheat, Sunflower and Ceanothus.

Look for it at Montezuma Vista Point, Kwaaymii Point and Garnet Peak.

Caterpillar Food Plants

BUCKTHORN FAMILY: Chaparral Whitethorn, *Ceanothus leucodermis* (below); Cupleaf Ceanothus, *C. greggii* (p. 89); Wedgeleaf Ceanothus, *C. cuneatus,* (p. 45); Hairy Ceanothus, *C. oliganthus* (not shown).

Chaparral Whitethorn, a common chaparral shrub 5'–13' tall, has whitish branches, alternate 3–veined evergreen leaves and pale blue to white flower clusters Mar–Jun.

SYLVAN HAIRSTREAK
Satyrium sylvinus
Size: Small (1"-1³/₈") *Flies:* May–Aug (1 flight)

Sylvan Hairstreak nectaring on Milkweed, a favorite nectar flower

The Sylvan Hairstreak is paler gray on the underside than the California Hairstreak (opposite page) and has fewer orange marginal spots. The upperside is also pale gray. The Sylvan's in our area are usually tailed.

Males commonly perch on but occasionally partrol around Willows, their caterpillar food plants, awaiting females. Adults nectar on flowers, especially on Milkweed.

Look for this chaparral butterfly near streams where willows and milkweeds grow.

Caterpillar Food Plants

WILLOW FAMILY: Slender Willow, *Salix exigua* (below & p. 82); Arroyo Willow, *Salix lasiolepis* (not shown).

Slender Willow, a streamside shrub 6' -15' tall, has male and female flowers on separate plants. The yellow unisexual catkins (male in this picture) bloom Mar-May.

CALIFORNIA HAIRSTREAK
Satyrium californica
Size: Small (1"-1¹/₄")   Flies: May–Aug (1 flight)

Garnet Peak SD Co, CA 20 May 1997

California Hairstreak nectaring on San Diego Sunflower in a chaparral burn area

The California Hairstreak has tails. Its gray-brown underside is darker than the Sylvan Hairstreak's (opposite page) with more orange submarginal spots. The gray-brown upperside hindwings have orange marks.

Look for California Hairstreaks nectaring at yellow chaparral composites—Sunflowers, San Diego Sunflower, Golden-Yarrow. Males perch and sometimes patrol.

They fly at such locales as Oriflamme Canyon, Kwaaymii Point and Garnet Peak.

Caterpillar Food Plants

BUCKTHORN FAM: Wedgeleaf Ceanothus, *Ceanothus cuneatus* (below). ROSE FAM: Mountain–Mahogany, *Cercocarpus betuloides* (right); Western Chokecherry, *Prunus virginiana* (p. 23). OAK FAM: Scrub Live Oak, *Quercus wislizeni* (p. 43). WILLOW FAM: *Salix* ssp (pp. 44, 82).

Chihuahua Valley SD Co, CA 4 May 2001

Wedgeleaf Ceanothus is a chaparral shrub 3'–8' tall with small, often wedge-shaped leaves. White or lavender flowers bloom Feb–Jun.

MOUNTAIN MAHOGANY HAIR-STREAK   *Satyrium tetra*
Size: Small (1"-1¹/₄")   Flies: May–Aug (1 flight)

Garnet Peak SD Co, CA 26 Jun 2000

Mountain Mahogany Hairstreak nectaring on Buckwheat

The Mountain Mahogany Hairstreak is gray on both sides with short tails and white-tipped fringes. The underside hindwing has a dark line edged with white. Over the gray is a dusting of white scales.

This chaparral hairstreak is easiest to find when nectaring at Buckwheat, often in small groups, or at Woolly Yarrow.

Look for the Mountain Mahogany Hairstreak at Oriflamme Canyon, Kwaaymii Point and Garnet Peak.

Caterpillar Food Plant

ROSE FAMILY: Mountain–Mahogany, *Cercocarpus betuloides* (below).

Culp Valley ABDSP, CA 21 Mar 1996

Mountain–Mahogany, a shrub or small tree 6'–25' tall of dry slopes, has dark green leaves toothed above the middle and clusters of small whitish flowers that bloom Apr–May.

45

'LOKI' JUNIPER HAIRSTREAK
Callophrys gryneus loki
Size: Tiny (⁷/₈"–1")   *Flies:* Feb–Oct (2-3 flights)

'Loki' Juniper Hairstreak, whose hindwings may also be greenish, sipping Desert Lavender

Loki is named for the troublemaker son of a Norse giant who plotted to kill a beloved god. Identify it by the underside pattern since it perches with wings folded. The upperside is plain brown. It has tails.

Loki flies near junipers—at Plum, Box and Bitter Creek Canyons and at Scissors Crossing/ San Felipe. It nectars on Sugarbush and Desert Lavender. Males perch for mates.

Nelson's Hairstreak (right) is similar but flies at higher elevations.

Caterpillar Food Plant
CYPRESS FAMILY: California Juniper, *Juniperus californica* (below).

California Juniper, an evergreen conifer, is 2'–15' high, sometimes to 40'. It has flat scalelike leaves. Berrylike seed cones, at first blue with a bloom, mature red-brown.

NELSON'S HAIRSTREAK
Callophrys nelsoni (= *C. gryneus nelsoni*)
Size: Small (1"–1¹/₈")   *Flies:* Apr–Sep (1 flight)

Nelson's Hairstreak with a purplish sheen nectaring on San Diego Goldenpea

The brown underside of Nelson's Hairstreak, visible when sitting, has tails and a purplish sheen when fresh. The upperside is brown. Though similar to its relative, Loki (left), it flies in montane coniferous forests where California Incensecedar grows. Males perch for females.

Look for Nelson's along the trail to Garnet Peak and in the Laguna Meadows nectaring on Buckwheat, San Diego Goldenpea and California Buttercup.

Caterpillar Food Plant
CYPRESS FAMILY: Incensecedar, *Calocedrus decurrens* (below).

California Incensecedar, an aromatic evergreen conifer, is a forest tree 50'–125' high with a conical crown. Branchlets of scaled leaves form flat sprays. Small cones are woody.

THICKET HAIRSTREAK
Callophrys spinetorum
Size: Small (1"–1¹/₄")   *Flies:* Mar–Aug (1–2 flts)

BROWN ELFIN
Callophrys augustinus
Size: Tiny–Sm (⁷/₈"–1¹/₈")   *Flies:* Jan–Aug (1 flt)

Thicket Hairstreak nectaring on Western Chokecherry

Brown Elfin nectaring on Desert Apricot

The red-brown underside of the Thicket Hairstreak has a vivid white line forming a W near the tail and a row of black dots running along the margin. The steel blue upperside must be seen in flight

Males perch on trees or shrubs on hilltops for females. Adults sip flowers and mud.

This hard-to-find butterfly flies in pinyon-juniper woodlands and montane coniferous forests where Dwarf Mistletoes, their caterpillar food plants, grow on pines.

The tailless Brown Elfin has brown undersides with faint dark markings. Hindwings are dark at the base, reddish brown at the margins. Uppersides are brown.

This widely distributed early spring butterfly has many food plants. Look for it at Culp Valley, Pinyon Ridge, the San Felipe areas, Garnet and Combs Peaks where it sips mud or flowers such as Desert Apricot, Deerweed, Sugarbush and Mulefat. Males perch on shrubs to await mates.

Caterpillar Food Plants

MISTLETOE FAMILY: Western Dwarf Mistletoe, *Arceuthobium campylopodum* (below); Pinyon Dwarf Mistletoe, *A. divaricatum* (not shown).

Some Caterpillar Food Plants

Many including BUCKTHORN FAM: Hollyleaf Redberry, *Rhamnus ilicifolia* (below); Hoary Coffeeberry, *R. tomentella* (p. 23); Cupleaf Ceanothus, *Ceanothus greggii* (p. 89); Chaparral Whitethorn, *C. leucodermis* (p. 44); ROSE FAM: Chamise, *Adenostoma fasciculatum* (p. 53).

Western Dwarf Mistletoe, parasitic on pines, has male and female flowers on separate plants in bloom Aug–Oct. Mature berries explode and seeds stick to branches.

Hollyleaf Redberry, a chaparral shrub up to 13' tall, has thick evergreen holly-shaped leaves with a spiny margin and tiny flowers Feb–Jun followed by small dark red berries.

47

BRAMBLE HAIRSTREAK
Callophrys perplexa (= *C. dumetorum p.*)
Size: Small (1"–1¹/₄")   *Flies:* Feb–May (1 flight)

Upper Tubb Canyon ABDSP, CA 5 Mar 2002

Bramble Hairstreak sipping Desert Sandmat

The Bramble, our only green tailless butterfly, is a lustrous green to blue-green on the underside hindwing. The intense color is caused by the interaction of light with microscopic structures of the wing scales (see p. 11). Male uppersides are gray, female are brown.

Look for this common spring flier from canyon bottoms to hilltops. Males perch to await mates. Fond of nectar, it sips flowers such as Desert Lavender, Desert Sandmat, Bladderpod, Desert Mistletoe, Desert Apricot, Deerweed and Buckwheat.

Caterpillar Food Plants

PEA FAMILY: Deerweed, *Lotus scoparius* (below & pp. 57, 59); Bishop's Lotus, *L. strigosus* (p. 32). BUCKWHEAT FAMILY: Tall Buckwheat, *Eriogonum elongatum* (p. 40); Buckwheat, *E. fasciculatum* (pp. 54, 59).

San Felipe–BLM SD Co, CA 20 Mar 2003

Deerweed, a broomlike bushy perennial 16"– 48" tall of dry slopes and desert washes, has yellow flowers in whorls around the stem bloom-Feb–Aug.

MALLOW SCRUB-HAIRSTREAK
Strymon istapa (= *columella*)
Size: Small (1"-1¹/₈")   *Flies:* Mar–Nov (sev flts)

Hellhole Canyon ABDSP, CA 5 May 1998

Mallow Scrub-Hairstreak perched on rock

The common name reflects the Mallow plants the caterpillar eats. Identify this butterfly by the pale gray underside with two dark spots near the body, its prominent band of dark spots and a tail with a black and orange spot near it. The upperside is dark gray-brown.

We have seen this uncommon butterfly twice, in Hellhole Canyon both in March sipping nectar at Everlastings and in May perched on a rock. Others have seen it flying at Laguna Meadows in May and fall.

Caterpillar Food Plant

MALLOW FAMILY: Rock Hibiscus, *Hibiscus denudatus* (below & p. 87).

Borrego Palm Canyon ABDSP, CA 3 Mar 2001

Rock Hibiscus, an attractive perennial 1'–2' tall of desert rocky slopes and canyons, has densely felted toothed leaves and whitish to lavender flowers Feb–May & Nov–Dec.

GRAY HAIRSTREAK
Strymon melinus

Size: Small (1"–1¼")   *Flies:* Jan–Dec (several flights)

Gray Hairstreak on Cryptantha

Hellhole Canyon ABDSP, CA 18 Mar 2003

The Gray Hairstreak, the most widespread hairstreak in the U.S., is a resident only in the warm west coast and south. But each spring it begins recolonizing the rest of the country. Its caterpiller can dine on a great variety of plants—over 50 species!

As its name implies it is gray. It has two tails, one long, one short, ornamented with an orange tail spot on both sides. On the underside it has a black and white line, usually edged in orange. Unlike most hairstreaks, it sometimes sits with wings open to display the dark blue-gray upperside. Male abdomens are orange, female are gray.

We see it in many locales—deserts, canyons, mountain tops. It sips nectar from Buckwheat, Sweetbush, Brittlebush, Mulefat and many others. Males perch to await mates, especially on hilltops such as Montezuma Vista Point.

Montezuma Vista Point ABDSP, CA 10 Mar 1997

Gray Hairstreak on Sugarbush, upperside

Some Caterpillar Food Plants and Caterpillars

Many including MINT FAM: Desert Lavender, *Hyptis emoryi* (below left). PEA FAM: Deerweed, *Lotus scoparius* (below center & pp. 48, 57, 59); Desert Cassia, *Senna armata* (below right & pp. 36, 37). MALLOW FAM: Rock Hibiscus, *Hibiscus denudatus* (pp. 48 & 87); Cheeseweed, *Malva parviflora* (pp. 77 & 94); Apricot Mallow, *Sphaeralcea ambigua* (pp. 77, 94 & 95). BUCKWHEAT FAM: Tall Buckwheat, *Eriogonum elongatum* (p. 40); Desert Trumpet, *E. inflatum* (p. 62); Knotty and/ or Foothill Buckwheat, *E. wrightii* ssp (p. 54). STONECROP FAM: Desert Dudleya, *D. saxosa* (p. 56).

Hellhole Canyon ABDSP, CA 2 Mar 2001

Culp Valley ABDSP, CA 25 May 2003

Senna Wash ABDSP, CA 7 May 2001

Desert Lavender, a shrub 3'–9' tall of desert washes and canyons, has fragrant felted leaves and clusters of violet flowers at branch tips Jan–Apr.

Gray Hairstreak Caterpillar on Deerweed. This caterpillar displays one of many color variations.

Gray Hairstreak Caterpillar eating Desert Cassia flowers, displaying another color variation.

49

LEDA MINISTREAK
Ministrymon leda
Size: Tiny (³/₄"–⁷/₈") *Flies:* Jan–Nov (sev flts)

Sentenac Canyon ABDSP, CA 11 Oct 1998

Leda Ministreak
Above: *sipping Alkali Golden-bush* Right: *winter form sipping Baccharis*

Sentenac Cienega 12 Oct 2003

Tiny Ledas have a pebbled underside with two tails, one short, one long. Hindwings have an orange-edged irregular line, short dots, dashes and an orange tail spot. The winter form *inez* is darker gray with less or no orange. Upperside wing bases are pale blue.

Ledas sip Alkali Goldenbush, Mesquite, Mulefat, Buckwheat, Baccharis. Males patrol or perch for females. Look for Ledas in Sentenac Cienega or in canyons near Mesquite.

Caterpillar Food Plant

PEA FAMILY: Honey Mesquite, *Prosopis glandulosa* (below).

Bitter Creek Can ABDSP, CA 28 Apr 2001

Honey Mesquite is a shrub to small tree up to 20' high of washes and sand dunes with dense cylindrical spikes of small sweet yellow flowers Mar–Jun.

MARINE BLUE
Leptotes marina
Size: Tiny (³/₄"–1") *Flies:* Jan–Dec (sev flts)

Upper Tubb Canyon ABDSP, CA 18 Oct 2003

Marine Blue nectaring on Butterweed

The Marine Blue has pale brown and white zebra bands on the underside; the hindwing has strong black metallic eyespots but no other black markings. On the upperside males are violet, females brown with blue.

This adaptable Blue flies in most habitats from low desert to mountain meadows. Males patrol in an erratic dancing flight around the food plants. They finally do stop--momentarily! Adults sip mud and many flowers—Catclaw, Buckwheat, Tall Buckwheat, Mesquite, Milkvine, Butterweed.

Some Caterpillar Food Plants

PEA FAM: Catclaw, *Acacia greggii* (below); False Indigo, *Amorpha fruticosa* (pp. 34, 88); Deerweed, *Lotus scoparius* (pp. 48, 57, 59); Honey Mesquite, *Prosopis glandulosa* (left); Screwbean Mesquite, *P. pubescens* (p. 51). ROSE FAM: Chamise, *Adenostoma fasciculatum* (p. 53).

Culp Valley ABDSP, CA 22 Jun 2000

Catclaw, a straggly shrub to small tree 12' tall, grows in desert washes and canyons. It has stout curved prickles on its branches and cylindrical spikes of yellow flowers Apr–Jun.

REAKIRT'S BLUE	CERAUNUS BLUE
Hemiargus (=*Echinargus*) *isola*	*Hemiargus ceraunus*
Size: Tiny (³/₄"–1") *Flies:* Mar–Oct (sev flts)	*Size:* Tiny (³/₄"–1") *Flies:* Feb–Nov (sev flts)

Reakirt's Blue nectaring on Buckwheat   *Ceraunus Blue on Catclaw*

Reakirt's and Ceraunus Blues, like the similar Marine Blue (opposite page), have one or more strong metallic black spots, sometimes called "eyes", on the underside hindwing margin. Reakirt's and Ceraunus also have two non-metallic black spots along the underside hindwing's top edge. To identify Reakirt's look for a row of submarginal white-ringed black spots on the underside forewing. Ceraunus does not have these spots. These three "eyed" Blues often fly together, with males patrolling around their Pea Family food plants.

Adults sip mud or moist sand and nectar at flowers—Filaree, Gilia, Buckwheat.

Look for Reakirt's Blue in Hellhole Canyon, Culp Valley and near Scissors Crossing around Mesquites and Catclaw.

This desert denizen sips flowers—Deerweed, Cryptantha, Indigo Bush, Desert Milkweed, Catclaw, Butterweed. Males sip mud.

Look for Ceraunus Blue in all desert and desert transition canyons and washes.

Some Caterpillar Food Plants

PEA FAMILY: Screwbean Mesquite, *Prosopis pubescens* (below left, right); Honey Mesquite, *P. glandulosa* (p. 50); Catclaw, *Acacia greggii* (p. 50).

Some Caterpillar Food Plants

PEA FAM: Screwbean Mesquite, *Prosopis pubescens* (below left, right); Honey Mesquite, *P. glandulosa* (p. 50); Catclaw, *Acacia greggii* (p. 50); Desert Rattlepod, *Astragalus crotalariae* (p. 32); Parish Locoweed, *A. douglasii* (p. 33); Palmer Locoweed, *A. palmeri* (p. 53). (Also see p. 109.)

Screwbean Mesquite, a deciduous tree 10'–30' tall with yellowish flowers in slender cylindrical spikes in bloom May–Jul, grows streamside and in other moist desert areas.

Screwbean Mesquite seedpods are distinctive. Mature coiled pods darken to brown. On dormant trees look for over-wintering seedpods hanging from twigs.

51

WESTERN PYGMY BLUE
Brephidium exile

Size: Tiny (¹/₂"–³/₄")   *Flies:* Jan–Dec (several flights)

Borrego Sink Borrego Springs, CA 24 Feb 1997

Western Pygmy Blue on Desert Thornbush

Our tiniest butterfly and the smallest in the U.S. Males, unlike most other blue species, and females have coppery brown uppersides with blue only near the body. The underside wings are bicolored coppery and gray with a marginal row of dark metallic eyespots on the hindwing.

We see the Pygmy Blue mainly in the deserts or desert transition where its major food plants, Saltbush or Desert Holly, grow—Badland washes, Borrego Sink, Yaqui Well, Sentenac Cienega.

Males patrol for mates around food and nectar plants. In dry years a whole colony may cluster around the only flowering shrub in sight to meet and mate as well as to nectar. These tiny Blues dart in and out of the shrub like busy blue bees.

Watch it visiting flowers such as Creosote, Orcutt's Aster, Sweetbush, Desert Thornbush, Desert Arrowweed, Alkali Goldenbush.

Cima, CA 10 Oct 2003

Western Pygmy Blue on Russian Thistle

Caterpillar Food Plants

GOOSEFOOT FAMILY: Desert Holly, *Atriplex hymenelytra* (below); Fourwing Saltbush, *A. canescens* (p. 92); California Goosefoot, *Chenopodium californicum* (p. 93); White Pigweed, *C. murale* (p. 93); Russian Thistle, *Salsola tragus* (above).

Coachwhip Canyon ABDSP, CA 2 Mar 2002

Coachwhip Canyon ABDSP, CA 5 Mar 2001

Desert Holly, an evergreen rounded shrub 1'–3' tall, grows in alkaline places including desert badland washes and canyons walls.

Desert Holly leaves are silvery-white and holly-like. Inconspicuous male and female flowers, which grow on different plants, bloom Jan–Apr.

WESTERN TAILED BLUE
Everes (= *Cupido*) *amyntula*
Size: Tiny–Sm (⅞"–1¼")   Flies: Jan–Sep (2 flts)

Western Tailed Blue on Yerba Mansa

Western Tailed Blues are the only blues in our region with tails. The underside is pale gray with small black spots; near the tail is a small orange spot. On the upperside the male is bright metallic blue, the female dark bluish-brown.

It flies low, visiting flowers and mud. Males patrol and perch for mates.

Look for this butterfly in moister habitats in open areas where its caterpillar food plants are found such as Sentenac Cienega, Culp Valley and Laguna Meadows.

Caterpillar Food Plants

PEA FAMILY: Palmer's Locoweed, *Astragalus palmeri* (below); Parish Locoweed, *A. douglasii* var. *parishii* (p. 33).

Palmer's Locoweed, a perennial of desert transition slopes has silvery pinnate leaves, purplish flowers Mar–May and inflated seed pods.

SPRING AZURE
Celastrina ladon echo (= *Celastrina echo*)
Size: Tiny–Sm (⅞"–1¼")   Flies: Jan–Dec (2 flts)

Spring Azure on Buckwheat

Spring Azures with a great variety of caterpillar food plants can live in a wide geographic range from Canada to Columbia.

The underside is light gray with faint dark spots and a row of crescents—vague to absent—along the margins. On the upperside the male is metallic azure blue, the female paler blue with dark borders.

Azures fly at higher elevations—Culp Valley, Kwaaymii Point, Garnet Peak. Males patrol and perch for mates and sip damp soil. Adults sip Buckwheat and Ceanothus.

Some Caterpillar Food Plants

Many including ROSE FAM Chamise, *Adenostoma fasciculatum* (below); BUCKTHORN FAMILY: Chaparral Whitethorn, *Ceanothus leucodermis* (p. 44); Hoary Coffeeberry, *Rhamnus tomentella* (p. 23). SUNFLOWER FAM: Mulefat, *Baccharis salicifolia* (p.14).

Chamise, an indicator species of chaparral, is an evergreen shrub 2'–12' high with bundles (fascicles) of small leaves on the stems and clusters of small white flowers Mar-Jul.

BERNARDINO DOTTED-BLUE
Euphilotes bernardino (=battoides b.)
Size: Tiny (³/₄"–⁷/₈") *Flies:* Feb–Aug (1 flt)

Bernardino Dotted-Blue at Buckwheat

'DAMMER'S' DOTTED-BLUE
Euphilotes enoptes dammersi
Size: Tiny (³/₄"–⁷/₈") *Flies:* Aug– Oct (1 flt)

'Dammer's' Dotted-Blue sips Knotty Buckwheat

The similar Bernardino and Dammer's Dotted-Blues do not fly together, simplifying identification. Both have orange bands on their underside hindwings (Bernardino's is usually more banded while Dammer's has individual spots) and non-metallic marginal black spots (versus metallic in Acmon and Lupine Blues, p. 59). Both male Dotted-blues have blue uppersides; both females are brownish with an orange band. Both species center their lives around the buckwheats their caterpillars eat. Males patrol around buckwheats. Females lay eggs on flower buds. Adults sip the flowers. Bernardino flies mostly late spring, 'Dammer's', mostly fall.

Look for the Bernardino Dotted-Blue, a more common blue with a widespread food plant, in Culp Valley, Scissors Crossing, San Felipe Valley, Box and Oriflamme Canyons.

Look for 'Dammer's' Dotted-Blue along the base of rocky canyon walls where its caterpillar food plants grow, such as Plum, Borrego Palm, Sentenac and Box Canyons.

Caterpillar Food Plant

BUCKWHEAT FAMILY: Buckwheat, *Eriogonum fasciculatum* (below & p. 59).

Buckwheat is a common shrub 1'–3' tall of rocky slopes and open areas. Bundles of small leaves alternate on the stems. Clusters of small white to pink flowers bloom Mar–Oct.

Caterpillar Food Plants

BUCKWHEAT FAM: Knotty Buckwheat, *Eriogonum wrightii* var *nodosum (*above & below left); Foothill Buckwheat, *E. w.* var *membranaceum* (below right); Tall Buckwheat, *E. elongatum* (p. 40).

Left: *'Dammer's' on Knotty Buckwheat,* a gray-woolly shrub 1'-3' tall of dry rocky places. Right: *Foothill Buckwheat,* shorter (8"–20") with green leaves. Both bloom Aug–Nov.

MOJAVE DOTTED-BLUE
Euphilotes mojave (= enoptes mojave)
Size: Tiny (³/₄"–⁷/₈")   *Flies:* Mar–Jun (1 flight)

Mojave Dotted-Blue, under-side

Indio, CA 26 Apr 1964 SDNHM

This desert butterfly that flies in Riverside County and north may fly in the most northern section of the Park. Undersides have an orange spotted band. Male uppersides are pale silvery-blue; female are brown often with extensive blue bases. Males patrol around Kidneyleaf Buckwheat (bottom right).

SMALL BLUE
Philotiella speciosa
Size: Tiny (⁵/₈"–³/₄")   *Flies:* Mar–Apr (1 flt)

Small Blue, under-side

Sweeney Pass 2 Apr 1960 SDNHM

Small Blues, closely related to Dotted-Blues, have no orange band. Undersides are gray with black dots. Male uppersides are blue, female brown. They fly in our area's southerly deserts —at Sweeney Pass and nearby In-Ko-Pah Gorge in Imperial Co. These spring Blues fly only after winters with adequate rainfall. Since many desert winters are dry, these tiny fliers, always inconspicuous as males patrol for mates just inches above the ground, are rarely seen.

Caterpillar Food Plant

For both Mojave Dotted-Blues and Small Blues —
BUCKWHEAT FAMILY: Kidneyleaf Buckwheat, *Eriogonum reniforme* (right).

Kidneyleaf Buckwheat, an annual only 2"–15" tall with felt-like kidney-shaped leaves and tiny yellow flowers Mar–Jun, grows in sandy desert washes.

'PRATT'S' DOTTED-BLUE
Euphilotes enoptes cryptorufes
Size: Tiny (³/₄"–⁷/₈")   *Flies:* May–Jun (1 flight)

'Pratt's' Dotted-Blue male, under-side

Baja CA Norte 2 June 1983 SDMNH

This rare subspecies, found so far only in the San Jacinto and Santa Rosa Mts. in Riverside Co. and in Baja California, has male underside orange bands darkened or even obliterated with black scales. Female bands may be darkened. Male uppersides are pale blue, female brown with blue bases and orange band.

Caterpillar Food Plant

BUCKWHEAT FAMILY: Davidson Buckwheat, *Eriogonum davidsonii* (below).

E A Monroe 2002 *Insert:* Garnet Pk 26 May '03

Davidson Buckwheat is an annual 2"–16" tall of dry slopes above 3000'. Its roundish leaves are wavy-edged. It has pinkish flowers May–Sep.

E A Monroe 2002 *Insert:* Hellhole Can 7 Mar 2003

SONORAN BLUE
Philotes sonorensis

Size: Tiny (⁷/₈"–1")   *Flies:* Jan–Jul (1 flight)

Plum Canyon ABDSP, CA 26 Feb 1999

Sonoran Blue male with red-orange patches only on the forewings sipping Desert Lavender

The light blue wings with red-orange patches makes the Sonoran Blue both beautiful and unmistakable.

Both males and females are shiny blue on the upperside. The sexes are easily separated. Females have a red-orange patch on upperside forewings and hindwings; males have red-orange patches only on the forewings. On the underside both sexes are gray with black markings and an orange patch on the forewing.

The Sonoran Blue favors cliffs and canyons where Desert Dudleya grows—Bitter Creek, Sentenac, Plum, Hellhole Canyons. Males patrol at the base of cliff walls for mates. Look for this early spring Blue sipping Desert Lavender, Sugarbush, Cryptantha.

Culp Valley ABDSP, CA 11 Mar 2003

Sonoran Blue female with a red-orange patch on all upperside wings

Plum Canyon ABDSP, CA 26 Mar 1999

Sonoran Blue, underside, sipping Desert Lavender

Caterpillar Food Plant and Egg

STONECROP FAMILY: Desert Dudleya, *Dudleya saxosa* (below & right).

Plum Canyon ABDSP, CA 18 Mar 1998

Desert Dudleya with two tiny eggs. This beautiful succulent of desert slopes with a rosette of fleshy narrow leaves grows nestled amidst rocks.

Plum Can 24 Feb '03

Sonoran Blue egg on Desert Dudley

Montezuma Vista Point ABDSP, CA 5 May 2001

Desert Dudleya in flower. Long red stalks bear reddish to yellowish flowers Apr–Jun.

56

SILVERY BLUE
Glaucopsyche lygdamus australis

Size: Small (1"–1¼")   *Flies:* Feb–Jul (1 flight)

Silvery Blue male on Sugarbush

In early spring if you see a fairly large Blue (for a Blue) flying rapidly up and down desert canyons and washes and flashing blue, it probably is a Silvery Blue male searching for a mate.

The genus name *Glaucopsyche* is from "glaucus," Latin for gray-blue, and "psyche," Greek for soul, to describe the upperside of males. Females are duller blue with wide dark borders. Identify this Blue by a single row of black dots rimmed with white on the gray underside.

Silvery Blues avidly sip flowers—Desert Mistletoe, Parish's Viguiera, Bladderpod, Mulefat, Desert Apricot, Desert Lavender, Sugarbush. Look for them flying in Borrego Palm, Hellhole, Bitter Creek, Box and Plum Canyons and at Culp Valley, Yaqui Well and Scissors Crossing/ San Felipe. Later check higher elevations.

Silvery Blue female

Silvery Blue, a mating pair, on bladderpod

Caterpillar Food Plants and Egg

PEA FAMILY: Deerweed, *Lotus scoparius* (below left & pp. 48, 59); Desert Lotus, *L. rigidus* (below right). Grape Soda Lupine, *L. excubitus* (p. 58); Adonis Lupine, *L. formosus* (p. 58); Parish Locoweed, *Astragalus douglasii* (p. 33).

Silvery Blue on Deerweed, its major food plant. This shrubby perennial with yellow flowers Feb-Aug grows in the desert washes the males patrol.

Silvery Blue egg on Deerweed

Desert Lotus, a desert perennial 1'– 3' tall, has two to three yellow pea flowers atop long stems Dec–May. Cylindrical pods are erect.

ARROWHEAD BLUE
Glaucopsyche piasus umbrosa
Size: Sm (1¹/₈"–1³/₈")   *Flies:* Apr–May (1 flight)

Laguna Meadows SD Co, CA 7 May 2001

Arrowhead Blue female laying an egg on Adonis Lupine

Arrowhead Blues, named for their underside band of white arrowheads pointing inward, also have a white spike. Uppersides are violet blue with dull brown borders in both sexes. Pale orange markings, near wing margins of both surfaces except male upperside forewings, are more extensive in females.

This subspecies *umbrosa* (shady), so named for its darkish underside, flies at Laguna Meadows. Males patrol near Adonis Lupines. Adults sip Tidytips and Filaree.

Caterpillar Food Plant & Egg

PEA FAMILY: Adonis Lupine, *Lupinus formosus* (below left).

Laguna Meadows SD Co, CA 7 May 2001

Laguna 7 May 2001

Egg on bud

Adonis Lupine, a perennial 8"–32" tall of pine forests and open slopes of montane meadows, has silky-haired palmate leaflets and showy wands of flowers Apr–Jul.

BOISDUVAL'S BLUE
Plebejus (= Icaricia) icarioides evius
Size: Sm (1¹/₈"–1³/₈")   *Flies:* Apr–Aug (1 flight)

Laguna Meadows SD Co, CA 27 Apr 2001

Boisduval's Blue nectaring on Meadowfoam

Boisduval's Blue has two rows of white-rimmed black dots on the underside, distinguishing it from the Silvery Blue with just one row of dots (p. 57). Males are pale metallic blue on the upperside, females brown with varying amounts of blue.

This Blue flies in the mountains where males patrol near their lupine caterpillar food plants. We find it along the Sunrise Highway and in the Laguna Meadows. Adults sip mud and Wild Onion or Meadowfoam.

Some Caterpillar Food Plants

PEA FAMILY: Grape Soda Lupine, *Lupinus excubitus* (below right); Adonis Lupine, *L. formosus* (below left).

Grape Soda Lupine, a perennial 8"–20" tall of pine forests and open slopes of montane meadows, has silky-haired palmate leaflets and wands of fragrant flowers Apr–Jul. Individual flower stalks, 1¹/₂"–2³/₈" long, are longer than Adonis's.

Doane Pond Palomar Mountain SP, CA 29 May 2003

ACMON BLUE	LUPINE BLUE
Plebejus (= *Icaricia*) *acmon*	*Plebejus* (= *Icaricia*) *lupini monticola*
Size: Tiny (³/₄"-1") *Flies:* Jan–Nov (sev flts)	*Size:* Tiny–Sm (⁷/₈"-1¹/₈") *Flies:* Mar–Jul (1 flt)

Acmon Blue male, upperside, on Deerweed *Lupine Blue male, upperside, on Cryptantha*

Acmon and Lupine Blues are hard to tell apart. Acmon has several flights. Both fly together during the Lupine's one spring/summer flight. Acmon is slightly smaller. On the upperside Acmon males are a paler lilac-blue, females usually brown though a spring form *cottlei* is blue. Lupine males are a deeper blue, females are brown to blue-green. Acmon has a narrower black margin on the upperside forewing than Lupine. Both have an upper- and underside orange band on the hindwing (Lupine's often with a bordering black line) and both have a marginal row of black metallic spots on the underside hindwing. Males patrol.

Acmon Blues sip mud and nectar at many plants— Deerweed, Desert Lavender, Desert Apricot, Tall Buckwheat. Look for Acmon in most habitats except low deserts.

Lupine Blues nectar especially at Buckwheat, but also at Cryptantha and Mountain Violets. Look for Lupine at Culp Valley, Oriflamme Canyon and Laguna Meadows.

Caterpillar and its Food Plants

PEA FAM: Miniature Lupine, *Lupinus bicolor* (below); Deerweed, *Lotus scoparius* (above & pp. 48, 57); Spanish Clover, *L. purshianus* (p. 60); Bishop Lotus, *L. strigosus* (p. 32) BUCKWHEAT FAM: Tall Buckwheat, *Eriogonum elongatum* (p. 40); Buckwheat, *E. fasciculatum* (below right & p. 54). (Also see p. 110.)

Caterpillar Food Plants

BUCKWHEAT FAM: Buckwheat, *Eriogonum fasciculatum* (below & p. 54); Knotty Buckwheat, *Eriogonum wrightii* var *nodosum* and/or Foothill Buckwheat, *E. w.* var *membranaceum* (both p. 54)

Left: *Caterpillar on Miniature Lupine tended by ants*
Milk Ranch Road Cuyamaca Rancho SP, CA 1 Jun 2003

Left: *Acmon female on Miniature Lupine*, a hairy annual 4"–16" tall of meadows and open slopes. Right: *Blue flowers* with white spots bloom Apr–Jun. Seed pods are hairy.

Lupine Blue female sipping Buckwheat, her caterpillar food plant. Buckwheat is a favorite nectar plant of many of our butterflies.

MELISSA BLUE
Lycaeides (= *Plebejus*) *melissa*

Size: Tiny-Small (⁷/₈"–1¹/₄")   *Flies:* Apr–Nov (probably 2 flights)

Melissa Blue

Melissa Blue is our only blue with orange bands on both the underside fore- and hind-wings. On the upperside males are blue with no bands, females brown with orange bands,

Males patrol all day near their caterpillar food plants in the Pea Family. Males sip mud and adults nectar at such plants as mustards and composites such as Pineapple Weed.

In our area Melissa Blue flies at higher elevations. Look for it at Kwaaymii Point, Laguna Meadows and around Lake Cuyamaca.

Caterpillar Food Plant

PEA FAMILY: Spanish Lotus, *Lotus purshianus* (right); Nevada Lotus, *L. nevadensis;* (p. 89); Parish Locoweed, *Astragalus douglasii* (p. 33); Grape Soda Lupine, *Lupinus excubitus* (p. 58).

Spanish Lotus is a multi-branched hairy annual about 4"–32" tall with leaflets usually in groups of three. Its attractive single pea flowers, whitish to pinkish tinged, bloom May–Oct. Look for it in dry or disturbed places at higher elevations.

Metalmarks (RIODINIDAE)

These small tropical butterflies, named for metallic flecks and patches on the wings of many species, are most common in Central and South America. Most U.S. species are shades of brown and orange, some with black and white markings, some with rows of metallic spots. Males do not use their greatly reduced two forelegs for walking. One of the four subfamilies, RIODININAE, occurs in the U.S. with 20 species. Five species fly here.

HABITS:
- Flight is rather swift and erratic.
- Adults feed on flower nectar.
- Males perch on branches to await females, though some species may also patrol.

CATERPILLAR FOOD PLANTS: Caterpillars in our area eat plants in the Buckwheat, Pea or Sunflower Families.

Eggs: Variable, but many have a flattened sea urchin shape.

Caterpillar (larva): Variable in color, often with long, fine hairs (setae), an unusual character among butterfly caterpillars. Some species are tended by ants as in the closely related Copper, Hairstreak and Blue Family. The ants apparently give protection from small predators in return for honeydew produced from glands.

Desert Metalmark

Chrysalis (pupa): Oval-shaped and rounded at both ends. Depending on species the chrysalis may hang from a support by tiny hooks (cremaster) at the end of the abdomen or may be hidden in ground litter.

Hibernation: Caterpillars hibernate in the temperate zones.

WRIGHT'S METALMARK
Calephelis wrighti

Size: Small (1"–1¹/₈")   *Flies:* Jan–Dec (several flights)

Wright's Metalmark

Wright's Metalmark, a fairly common desert butterfly of rocky slopes and rocky washes, has a reddish brown upperside that displays a milky sheen in fresh individuals. The underside is yellow-orange. Both upper and undersides have 2 narrow dark metallic bands, more noticeable on the underside. Also note the white-checkered fringes and the wavy outer margin of the forewing.

You usually will find Wright's Metalmark near its caterpillar food plant Sweetbush. Adults nectar on Sweetbush. Males perch on or near Sweetbush to await females and occasionally may patrol around this shrub.

Look for Wright's in desert washes and canyons such as Borrego Palm, Hellhole, Upper Tubb, Box and Plum Canyons.

Wright's Metalmark on Sweetbush

Caterpillar Food Plant and Caterpillar

SUNFLOWER FAMILY: Sweetbush, *Bebbia juncea* (below).

Sweetbush is a desert shrub about 2'–5' tall and often broader that grows along rocky slopes and washes. The golden disk flowers, which attract many insects, bloom Jan–Jul.

Wright's Metalmark caterpillar, tiny with luxuriant white hairs, eats the thin greenish epidermal layer of the nearly leafless rush-like branches of Sweetbush.

61

DESERT METALMARK
Apodemia mejicanus deserti (= *A. mormo deserti*)

Size: Tiny–Small (⅞"-1¼")   *Flies:* Feb–Nov (2 – several flights)

Hellhole Canyon ABDSP, CA 24 Mar 1997

Desert Metalmark nectaring on Sweetbush

The Desert Metalmark, also called the Sonoran Metalmark, is a true desert denizen in our area. On the upperside the forewings have a burnt orange base and dark border with white spots; the hindwings are mostly dark gray with white spots unlike the similar Behr's and 'Peninsular' Metalmarks (opposite) which have an orange band on the hindwings. The underside hindwings are dark gray with white spots.

Adults nectar at Brittlebush, Desert Lavender, and Sweetbush. Males perch on various low shrubs near Desert Trumpet awaiting females.

Look for it from early spring to late fall in such areas as the Visitor Center, Yaqui Well and in most of the desert washes and canyons— Borrego Palm, Surprise, Hellhole, Plum, Box and Bow Willow.

Hellhole Canyon ABDSP, CA 4 Apr 1996

Desert Metalmark, underside, sipping Brittlebush

Caterpillar Food Plants and Caterpillar

BUCKWHEAT FAMILY: Desert Trumpet, *Eriogonum inflatum* (left & below); probably Buckwheat, *E. fasciculatum* (pp. 54, 59).

Borrego Springs, CA 8 Mar 2003

Tubb Can Rd Borrego Springs, CA 15 Mar 2000

Tubb Can Rd Borrego Springs, CA 8 May 2001

Desert Trumpet with its distinct inflated stems and basal leaves is a desert annual or perennial 8"–40" high.

Desert Trumpet's tiny yellow flowers on long stems bloom Mar–Oct.

Desert Metalmark caterpillar on Desert Trumpet. Notice how the caterpillar is chewing the epidermis of the stem.

BEHR'S METALMARK
Apodemia virgulti (= *A. mormo virgulti*)
Size: Tiny–Sm (⁷/₈"–1¹/₄") *Flies:* Jan–Dec (sev flts)

Culp Valley ABDSP, CA 21 Mar 2002

Behr's Metalmark
Above: *sipping Narrowleaf Goldenbush*
Right: *on Buckwheat*

San Felipe, CA 5 May 2001

Behr's has prominent orange areas on the upperside of *all* wings with dark borders and white spots.It flies at higher elevations than the Desert Metalmark, in desert transition and chaparral—San Felipe and Culp Valleys, Pinyon Ridge, Kwaaymii Point.
　　Males perch on Buckwheat awaiting females. Adults sip Narrowleaf Goldenbush.

Caterpillar Food Plant
BUCKWHEAT FAMILY: Buckwheat, *Eriogonum fasciculatum* (pp. 54, 59).

PALMER'S METALMARK
Apodemia palmeri
Size: Tiny–Sm (³/₄"–1¹/₈") *Flies:* Mar–Nov (sev flts)

Sentenac Cienega ABDSP, CA 11 Oct 1998

Palmer's Metalmark perched on Alkali Goldenbush.
Above: *Upperside*
Right: *Underside*

ABDSP, CA 11 Oct 1998

　　Palmer's brown upperside has orange margins, white spots. The underside is pale orange and white.
　　Adults sip flowers such as Mulefat and Alkali Goldenbush. Males perch on or near Mesquites, their caterpillar food plants. Look for this uncommon butterfly around Mesquites in desert and desert transition.

Caterpillar Food Plants
PEA FAM: Honey Mesquite, *Prosopis glandulosa* (p. 50); Screwbean Mes., *P. pubescens* (p. 51).

'PENINSULAR' MORMON METALMARK
Apodemia mormo peninsularis
Size: Tiny–Small (⁷/₈"-1¹/₈")　　　　　　　　*Flies:* Apr-Jun (1 flight)

'Peninsular' Metalmark sipping Meadowfoam
Near right: *Upperside*
Far right: *Underside*

　　This newly named subpecies flies in montane Jeffrey Pine forests such as Laguna Meadows, while the similar Behr's flies in chaparral. Upperside forewings have more orange scaling than Behr's and two center white spots of the postmedian row are reduced in size.

Laguna Meadows SD Co, CA 9 May 2000

Laguna Meadows SD Co, CA 9 May 2000

Caterpillar Food Plant
BUCKWHEAT FAM: Foothill Buckwheat, *Eriogonum wrightii* var *membranaceum* (p. 54).

Brushfoots (NYMPHALIDAE)

Members of this large and varied family of mainly medium-sized butterflies have the front pair of legs in both sexes reduced in size to become small and brush-like, hence, the name Brushfoots for this family. These brush "feet" possess scent receptors for detecting food plants. Female Snouts, which have normal legs, are the only exception. Of about 185 species in the U.S., 28 species occur in our region.

HABITS:

* Flight behavior is variable depending upon the species; some species migrate with the most famous being the Monarch and the Painted Lady.
* Many species feed at flower nectar. Others prefer sap, rotting fruit, animal dung and carrion.
* Males locate mates by perching or patrolling depending upon the species.

Egg: Often ribbed and laid singly or in clusters or columns on its food plant, or sometimes only nearby.

Caterpillar (larva): Variable in shape, many species have rows of bristly tubercles or branching spines while others have only scattered short hairs. Some species are solitary feeders. Other species feed communally during the early growth stages.

Chrysalis (pupa): In most species the chrysalis is suspended from a silk mat by hooks at the end of the abdomen. The chrysalis may be ornamented with tubercles and metallic spots.

Hibernation: Over half the species in our region over-winter as caterpillars, the rest as adults.

SIX SUBFAMILIES occur in our region:

SNOUTS (LIBYTHEINAE): The only species in this subfamily that flies in the U.S. is an uncommon migrant in our area or possibly occurs in scattered colonies where hackberry trees grow. Snout butterflies may migrate in vast numbers. The Snout is named for its extraordinarily long palpi (mouth-parts) that appear as a long nose or snout having no obvious function except as camouflage. When at rest on a twig with wings folded, it looks like a leaf with the long nose resembling the leaf petiole. **PLANTS EATEN BY THE CATERPILLARS** are hackberries in the Elm Family.

American Snout

LONGWINGS (HELICONIINAE): Named for the elongate wings of some tropical Longwings such as the migrant Gulf Fritillary in our region. Thirty-seven species occur in the U.S. Our two resident species and two migrant species, all called Fritillaries, are medium to large, mainly orange and often with showy silver or white spots on their under hindwing. **PLANTS EATEN BY THE CATERPILLARS** are Mountain Violets for our two resident species. Both migrants eat Passionflowers (often planted as ornamentals); one also eats violets and other plants.

Coronis Fritillary

TRUE BRUSHFOOTS (NYMPHALINAE): This large varied subfamily with about 90 species in the U.S. and 17 species in our area are mostly small to medium butterflies with predominant colors of orange, brown and black. **PLANTS EATEN BY THE CATERPILLARS** are diverse. Most species limit their diet to just one plant family. The outstanding exception, Painted Ladies, eat plants in many families.

California Patch

SATYRS (SATYRINAE): Like mythical woodland deities, Satyrs are fond of shaded forest areas. Typically they fly with a nymph-like skip and dance. Usually medium-sized, in muted shades of brown, orange or yellow, they often have one or more marginal eyespots. With their short probosises they rarely nectar at flowers, but prefer to feed on sap, dung or rotting fruit. Of the 45 species in the U.S., two species fly in our area. **PLANTS EATEN BY THE CATERPILLARS** are grasses, while all other Brushfoots eat dicots.

Common Ringlet

ADMIRALS & RELATIVES (LIMENITIDINAE): Our two species of these handsome, mid-sized butterflies have broad white wing bands. Most Admirals fly with a flap and glide style. About 30 species occur in the U.S. with two in our area. **PLANTS EATEN BY THE CATERPILLARS** are in the Oak, Rose and Willow Families.

California Sister

MILKWEED BUTTERFLIES (DANAINAE): These tropical butterflies, unable to withstand freezing during any life cycle stage, must winter in frost-free areas of the U.S. where three resident species plus one rare migrant occur. Our two species, the Monarch and the Queen, the royal couple, migrate north in the summer. Monarchs also migrate south in the fall. In California they winter in several sites along the Pacific Coast. There is even a report of overwintering one year in Anza-Borrego Desert State Park! **PLANTS EATEN BY THE CATERPILLARS** are in the Milkweed Family.

Queen

65

AMERICAN SNOUT
Libytheana carinenta

Size: Sm–Med (1³/₈"–1⁷/₈")   *Flies:* usually Sep–Oct (1 flight)

Cima, CA 21 Oct 2003

American Snout

The American Snout is uncommon here. Look for it near Netleaf Hackberry. Identify it by square wingtips and long snout-like palpi (mouthparts). When perched with wings closed on a twig, it appears like a dead leaf. See p. 64 for the orange, brown and white upperside.

Caterpillar Food Plant

ELM FAMILY: Netleaf Hackberry, *Celtis reticulata* (below).

Centennial Cone Gilpin Co, CO 8 Jul 2001

The spreading Netleaf Hackberry 6–30' tall has rough toothed deciduous leaves with a strong network of veins on the underside. It grows in isolated canyons, seeps or washes.

VARIEGATED FRITILLARY
Euptoieta claudia

Size: Medium (1³/₄"–2¹/₄")   *Flies:* Jun–Oct (2 flts)

Rocky Mountain NP, CO 4 Aug 1997

Variegated Fritillary Above: **upperside** Right: **underside**

Boulder Co, CO 17 Jul 2001

Variegated Fritillaries at times fly here, as three we saw flying west of Cuyamaca Lake. Uppersides are orange to brown with black marks. Undersides are tannish brown with pale patches but no silver spots.

Caterpillar Food Plant

VIOLET FAMILY: Violets, *Viola* spp (p. 67). Possibly other plants and families.

CALLIPPE FRITILLARY
Speyeria callippe comstocki

Size: Med–Large (2"–2¹/₂")   *Flies:* Apr–Aug (1 flt)

Ventura Co, CA 4 Jun 1935 U of CO Mus

Callippe Fritillary Above: **upperside** Right: **underside**

Ventura Co, CA 4 Jun 1935

Callippe, not as common as Coronis (opposite) here, is more tannish, less bright orange. Callippe's underside hindwing marginal silvery spots are triangular whereas Coronis' are more rounded.

Caterpillar Food Plant

VIOLET FAMILY: Mountain Violet, *Viola purpurea* (p. 67).

CORONIS FRITILLARY
Speyeria coronis semiramis

Size: Medium–Large (2"–2⅝")   *Flies:* May–Oct (1 flight)

Cuyamaca Rancho SP, CA 24 Jun 2000

Coronis Fritillary nectaring on buckwheat

We find this gorgeous fritillary at higher elevations, Kwaaymii Point, Garnet Peak, the Cuyamacas. Watch for Coronis swooping in to nectar at Buckwheat.

Its upperside is bright golden orange. The underside forewing has a reddish flush except near the wing tip; the hindwing displays silvery spots with marginal spots somewhat rounded. These silvery spots characteristic of the *Speyeria* genus (sometimes called the Silverspots) are caused by scale structures (see p. 11). Males patrol for mates. Adults sip moist sand or mud and nectar.

Interestingly, Coronis females do not lay eggs upon violet plants, since they grew earlier in the spring and have now dried up and disappeared. Rather, they lay eggs in the vicinity of where spring violets grew. Eggs overwinter. Caterpillars hatching from eggs the following spring will somehow find fresh growing violets for dining. Other fritillaries of dry climates such as Callippe (opposite page) lay eggs in the same way.

The **Gulf Fritillary** (p. 105), another Longwing whose caterpillars eat Passionflower, is a stray.

Cuyamaca Rancho SP, CA 24 Jun 2000

Coronis Fritillaries, mating pair

Caterpillar Food Plant

VIOLET FAMILY: Mountain Violet, *Viola purpurea* (below).

Garnet Peak Trail SD Co, CA 4 May 2000

Laguna Meadows SD Co, CA 27 Apr 2001

Mountain Violets, 1"–9" high, grow on the shaded floor of the Montane Coniferous Forest. The simple leaves are usually green with a purple tinge.

The beautiful Mountain Violet flower is yellow with purplish veins. The upper two petals are purplish on the underside. It blooms Apr–Jun.

67

TINY CHECKERSPOT
Dymasia dymas imperialis

Size: Tiny–Small (⁷/₈"–1¹/₄")   *Flies:* Jan–Nov (several flights)

Senna Wash ABDSP, CA 2 May 1998

Tiny Checkerspot nectaring on Desert Cassia

Our smallest checkerspot, the dainty Tiny Checkerspot, is orange with a black network on the upperside; the leading edge of the forewing has a pale spot. The underside hindwing has orange and white bands. Look for it in desert washes and canyons—Senna Wash, Hellhole, Borrego Palm, Plum and Bitter Creek Canyons. With sufficient winter/spring rains, they may flutter in abundance around Chuparosa.

Senna Wash ABDSP, CA 2 May 1998

Males never fly very far before stopping to perch and then soon taking off again. You can often follow their low fluttering flight and closely approach them after they alight on a nearby twig or on a flower for nectar.

Favorite nectar flowers include Desert Pincushion, Brittlebush, Parish Viguiera, Sweetbush and Desert Cassia.

Tiny Checkerspot sipping Sweetbush

Caterpillar Food Plant and Caterpillar

ACANTHUS FAMILY: Chuparosa, *Justicia californica* (below and right).

Bitter Creek Canyon ABDSP, CA 28 Apr 2001

Hellhole Canyon ABDSP, CA Apr 1991

Chuparosa, a subshrub of desert washes, has arching often leafless branches growing 1'–5' long. The small ovate leaves are early deciduous. It blooms Feb-Jun, in the fall after summer rain.

Tiny Checkerspot caterpillar on Chuparosa. The red flower petals are joined into a tubular 2–lipped corolla about 1"–1¹/₄" long.

68

CALIFORNIA PATCH
Chlosyne californica

Size: Small–Medium (1¼"–1⅞")   *Flies:* Feb–Nov (several flights)

California Patch on Parish Viguiera

The California Patch, an attractive desert butterfly in Halloween garb with its contrasty pattern of orange and dark brown banding on both surfaces, is commonly seen flying near Parish Viguiera in our desert/desert transition washes and canyons such as Hellhole, Plum and Box Canyons and San Felipe/Scissors Crossing. Also look on hilltops such as Montezuma Vista Point where males perch awaiting females.

You may be able to approach closely as it sips Parish Viguiera, Sweetbush, Desert Lavender, Fernleaf Phacelia or Bishop Lotus.

If you inspect leaves or stems of Parish Viguiera, you may find several small black, spiny caterpillars feeding communally as do other species in this genus. Older, larger caterpillars disperse to feed by themselves.

California Patch, underside, perching on Jojoba on a hilltop

Hellhole Canyon ABDSP, CA 1 May 2001

San Felipe/ Scissors Crossing ABDSP, CA 31 May 2003

Caterpillar Food Plants, Caterpillar and Chrysalis

SUNFLOWER FAMILY: Parish Viguiera, *Viguiera parishii* (below & p. 70); occasionally Western Sunflower, *Helianthus annuus* (p. 70).

Hellhole Canyon ABDSP, CA 19 Mar 2000

Parish Viguiera, a compact desert shrub 12"–30" tall with triangular large-toothed rough leaves and yellow flowers Jan–Jun, grows on dry rocky slopes or along washes.

Hellhole Canyon ABDSP, CA 1 Mar 2002

California Patch caterpillar on Parish Viguiera

Hellhole Canyon ABDSP, CA 8 Mar 2002

California Patch chrysalis on Parish Viguiera

69

BORDERED PATCH
Chlosyne lacinia crocale
Size: Sm –Med (1³/₈"–2") *Flies:* Mar–Oct (sev flts)

GABB'S CHECKERSPOT
Chlosyne gabbii
Size: Sm–Med (1¹/₄"–1³/₄") *Flies:* Mar–Sep (1 flt)

Sonny Bono Salton Sea NWR, CA 16 Oct 2003

Upper Oriflamme Can ABDSP, CA 21 May 1997

Bordered Patch
Above: *sipping West. Sunflower*
Right: *underside*

Sonny Bono Salton Sea NWR, CA

The Bordered Patch usually flies in cultivated areas with roadside sunflowers east of our area. Occasionally it strays here, most commonly in the fall. Sometimes it flies with its close relative, the California Patch (p. 69).

Individuals in this highly variable species are black on the upperside with an orange, cream or white band, sometimes narrow or absent, across the hindwing. The underside hindwing is black with a cream band and marginal cream spots.

Gabb's Checkerspot female
Above: *upperside*
Right: *underside*

Combs Peak SD Co. CA 4 May '01

Gabb's Checkerspot females are more contrasty, less uniformly orange checkered, than males. In our area Gabb's may be confused with Neumoegen's Checkerspot (opposite) that has narrower black lines and flies in deserts. We find Gabb's at higher elevations such as Upper Oriflamme Canyon, and near Garnet Peak and Combs Peak though not a hilltopper. It nectars on sunflowers and cryptantha and sips mud. Males sip dung.

Caterpillars & their Food Plants
SUNFLOWER FAMILY: Parish Viguiera, *Viguiera parishii* (p. 69); Western Sunflower, *Helianthus annuus* (above, below).

Caterpillar Food Plants
SUNFLOWER FAMILY: Cudweed Aster, *Lessingia filaginifolia* (below); Sawtooth Goldenbush, *Hazardia squarrosa* (p. 15).

Sonny Bono Salton Sea NWR, CA 16 Oct 2003

Bordered Patch Caterpillars on Western Sunflower, colonial and variable, are orange to black.

Garnet Peak Trail SD, Co, CA 13 Oct 2003

Cudweed Aster, an erect perennial under 3' tall, has elongate leaves, violet flowers with yellow centers Jun–Oct.

'NEUMOEGEN'S' SAGEBRUSH CHECKERSPOT
Chlosyne acastus neumoegeni

Size: Medium (1¹/₂"–1³/₄")   *Flies:* Mar–Jun; Aug–Nov (2 flights)

*'Neumoegen's' Sagebrush
Checkerspot on Orcutt's Aster*

'Neumoegen's' flies mainly in the Mojave Desert, less often in our desert canyons and badlands. Occasionally we see it flying or sipping Brittlebush or Sweetbush in Hellhole or Plum Canyon in spring or sipping Butterweed in Culp Valley in fall. Early one March in the Coachwhip Canyon badlands, we found several caterpillars eating Orcutt's Aster.

Neumoegen's is orange like Gabb's (opposite) but has narrower, less prominent black lines on the upperside. Also Gabb's flies at higher elevations.

Males perch or may patrol for females.

Like other checkerspots Neumoegen's lays eggs in clusters. The caterpillars feed communally and then enter diapause when half-grown. After diapause they resume feeding and form chrysalises. They then emerge as adults about two weeks later.

*'Neumoegen's' Sagebrush Checkerspot,
underside*

Coachwhip Canyon ABDSP, CA 21 Mar 2001

Coachwhip Canyon ABDSP, CA 21 Mar 2001

Caterpillar Food Plants

SUNFLOWER FAMILY: Desert Goldenhead, *Acamptopappus sphaerocephalus* (below left); Orcutt's Aster, *Xylorhiza orcuttii* (below right).

Sentenac Cienega ABDSP, CA 27 May 2003

Coachwhip Canyon ABDSP, CA 5 Mar 2001

Desert Goldenhead is a rounded desert shrub 8"–3' tall with golden disk flowers Dec–May.

Orcutt's Aster, 1'–3' tall with showy purple flowers Feb–Apr, grows in arid canyons and badlands.

Caterpillar and Chrysalis

Below: *'Neumoegen's' Sagebrush Checkerspot caterpillar on Orcutt's Aster*

Coachwhip ABDSP 7 Mar 2001

Coachwhip ABDSP Mar 2001

Left: *'Neumoegen's' Sagebrush Checkerspot chrysalis*

71

LEANIRA CHECKERSPOT
Chlosyne (=Thessalia) leanira wrighti
Size: Small–Medium (1³/₈"–1³/₄")   *Flies:* Mar–Jun (1 flight); occasionally in fall after summer rains

Culp Valley ABDSP, CA 8 Apr 1996

Culp Valley ABDSP, CA 8 Apr 1996

**Leanira Checkerspot
on Woolly Indian Paintbrush**

A distinctive heavy black chain on the creamy underside hindwing distinguishes Leanira from all similar checkerspots in our area. The vivid upperside is red-orange, cream and black. The forewings are more rounded than Henne's (opposite) and the black abdomen has white rings instead of dots.

Look for Leanira, not easy to find, on rocky ridge tops near Montezuma Vista Point where hilltopping males patrol with frequent stops to perch atop a convenient flowerhead or shrub. At Culp Valley look for females near Woolly Paintbrush or males sipping mud. In Lower Oriflamme Canyon Leanira sips Narrowleaf Goldenbush.

Leanira Checkerspot on Sugar-bush. Notice the black "chain."

Caterpillar Food Plant
SNAPDRAGON FAMILY: Woolly Indian Paintbrush, *Castilleja foliolosa* (below).

Culp Valley ABDSP, CA 11 Mar 2003

San Felipe Valley-BLM   SD Co, CA 26 Feb 2000

Woolly Indian Paintbrush is a subshrub 10"–18" high, felt-like in appearance with linear leaves that are sometimes lobed. It grows on rocky dry slopes in desert transition and on the edges of chaparral.

Woolly Indian Paintbrush with brilliant bracts overshadowing the tiny flowers that bloom Feb–Jun.

'HENNE'S' VARIABLE CHECKERSPOT
Euphydryas chalcedona hennei

Size: Small–Medium (1¼"–2¼")   *Flies:* Mar–Apr (1 flight); occasionally in fall after summer rains

'Henne's' Variable Checkerspot

In our area the *hennei* subspecies of this highly variable species flies in desert and desert transition canyons.

Recognize 'Henne's' Checkerspot by its striking white and red checkering with black bordering and veins and pointed forewings. White dots along the sides of the black abdomen distinguish it from the similiar Leanira (opposite) with white rings and from Quino (p. 74) with no dots or rings.

Males patrol along canyon washes in Hellhole and Sentenac Canyons, Culp Valley, Jacumba and the San Felipe Valley, stopping to perch briefly. Adults sip flowers such as Desert Lavender, Narrowleaf Goldenbush, Desert Yellowhead and Mulefat.

'Henne's' Variable Checkerspot perching on Desert Lotus

Caterpillar Food Plants

SNAPDRAGON FAMILY: Desert Bushpenstemon, *Keckiella antirrhinoides* (below). Woolly Indian Paintbrush, *Castilleja foliolosa* (p. 72).

Desert Bushpenstemon is a shrub 2'–8' tall which grows on rocky slopes in desert and especially desert transition habitats. This variety has small hoary leaves.

***Desert Bushpenstemon* with showy yellow snapdragon-like flowers** that bloom Apr–May. Note the hairy staminode or "beardtongue," a penstemon characteristic.

73

QUINO CHECKERSPOT
Euphydryas editha quino
Size: Sm–Med (1¼"–2")   *Flies:* Feb–Jun (1 flt)

Culp Valley ABDSP CA 24 Mar 2002

Quino Checker-spot Above: *sipping Mulefat* Right: *San Diego Natural History Museum Baja field trip*

Baja CA, Mex 2 Apr '95

Quino is an uncommon subspecies federally listed as endangered. It occurs in scattered colonies in San Diego County in desert transition/chaparral habitat. We have seen one Quino in the Park, nectaring on Mulefat. Males hilltop for mates.

Easily confused with Henne's Checkerspot (preceding page), Quino is more orange-brown, less reddish. The forewings are more rounded and it has no white dots on the abdomen.

Caterpillar Food Plants

PLANTAIN FAM: Southwestern Plantain, *Plantago patagonica* (below & p. 80). SNAPDRAGON FAM: White Snapdragon, *Antirrhinum coulterianum* (p. 80); Purple Owl's-Clover, *Castilleja exserta* (p. 80).

Jacumba ABDSP, CA 25 Apr 2001

Southwestern Plantain. The hairy flower spike has long basal bracts below tiny white flowers Apr–Jun.

MYLITTA CRESCENT
Phyciodes mylitta
Size: Small (1⅛"–1½")   *Flies:* Feb–Nov (sev flts)

Garnet Peak SD Co, CA 20 May 1997

Mylitta Crescent Above: *female upperside* Right: *male underside*

Culp Valley ABDSP 17 May 1997

Mylitta, our only resident Crescent, can be recognized by the white crescent mark near the margin of the underside hindwing. On the upperside males are more uniform orange than females.

Mylitta tends to occur locally. We find Mylitta in Hellhole and Upper Oriflamme Canyons, Culp Valley and Garnet Peak.

It sips mud and nectars at composites, including the beautiful San Diego Sunflower. Males patrol and perch for mates.

Caterpillar Food Plants

SNAPDRAGON FAMILY: Seep Monkeyflower, *Mimulus guttatus* (below). SUNFLOWER FAMILY: Thistles, *Cirsium* spp (not shown).

Culp Valley ABDSP CA 1 May 2000

Seep Monkey-flower, a perennial 1'–2' tall of wet places, has bright yellow flowers, often with red-dotted throats, Apr–Aug.

SATYR COMMA
Polygonia satyrus
Size: Med (1³/₄"–2¹/₄") *Flies:* Jan–Nov (1 flight)

Culp Valley ABDSP, CA 9 Apr 1996

Culp Valley ABDSP, CA 9 Apr 1996

Above top: *Satyr Comma sipping mud*
Above: *Notice the comma on the underside*

Butterflies in this *Polygonia* genus have jagged wing margins, hence giving this group the name Anglewings. They also have a white mark resembling a comma or questionmark on the underside hindwing. The Satyr Comma shows a silver comma.

Satyrs seldom visit flowers, preferring to sip mud, damp sand, rotted fruit and sap. Males perch to await females. They are long-lived with adult butterflies over-wintering.

This butterfly is not common in our area. It prefers moist, cool, shady habitats. We see it in riparian locales where Hoary Nettles grow such as at Scissors Crossing, Sentenac Cienega and Culp Valley.

Caterpillar Food Plant
NETTLE FAMILY: Hoary Nettle, *Urtica dioica* ssp *holosericea* (right).

RED ADMIRAL
Vanessa atalanta
Size: Med (1³/₄"–2¹/₄") *Flies:* Jan–Dec (2 flts)

Sentenac Cienega ABDSP, CA 3 Mar 2000

Red Admiral

A cosmopolitan butterfly, the active and fast-flying Red Admiral is widespread in North America though not common here. Its dark wings with bright red-orange bands and white spots are unique.

We see this riparian butterfly in early spring and in fall at Sentenac Cienega and Culp Valley where Hoary Nettles grow.

Not so fond of flowers, it visits mainly sap, fruit and dung. Males perch on bushes or the ground to await females. Adults overwinter in our mild area.

Caterpillar Food Plant
NETTLE FAMILY: Hoary Nettle, *Urtica dioica* ssp *holosericea* (below).

Culp Valley ABDSP, CA 23 Jun 2000

Hoary Nettle, a streamside perennial with erect unbranched stems 4'–10' tall and long leaves covered with hairs, some stinging, has wind-pollinated flowers Jun–Sep.

PAINTED LADY
Vanessa cardui

Size: Medium–Large (2"–2¹/₂")   *Flies:* Jan–Dec (several flights)

Upper Tubb Canyon ABDSP, CA 12 Mar 2001

Painted Lady nectaring on Desert Apricot

The best known butterfly in Borrego Springs! In years of heavy winter rains, they can not be ignored as they pass through town in a northward migration. Busy roads become littered with bodies of the dead and wounded. But unlike the Monarch migration, this Lady has few return flights southward. In our mild climate it can live year-round.

Unlike most butterflies whose caterpillars favor only a few food plants, the Painted Lady has a catholic taste for many plants—including thistles (its species name *cardui* is Latin for thistle). Its undiscerning appetite helps explain why this Lady, the world's most widespread butterfly, is often called the Cosmopolitan.

Males perch for females. In wet years flowers may teem with nectaring adults.

Two similar Ladies fly in our region. To tell them apart see descriptions on pp. 77 & 78.

Mountain Palm Springs ABDSP, CA 11 Oct 1995

Painted Lady sipping Alkali Goldenbush

Some Caterpillar Food Plants, Egg, Caterpillar and Chrysalis

Many including: PEA FAMILY: Indigobush, *Psorothamnus schottii* (below left); Arizona Lupine, *Lupinus arizonicus* (below right). BORAGE FAMILY: Fiddleneck, *Amsinkia tessellata* (below top center & pp. 15, 30). MALLOW FAMILY: Cheeseweed, *Malva parviflora* (pp. 77, 94). NETTLE FAMILY: Hoary Nettle, *Urtica dioica* (p. 75). (Also see p. 111.)

ABDSP, CA 27 Mar '03

Caterpillar on Fiddleneck

Below: *Egg on Arizona Lupine*
Right: *Chrysalis*

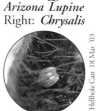

Hellhole Can 18 Mar '03

Borrego Springs, CA 12 Mar 2001

Near Bow Willow ABDSP, CA 25 Apr 2001

Indigobush, a spiny shrub 3'–9' tall of bajadas and sandy washes, has blue to purple blooms Mar–May.

Hoberg Canyon ABDSP, CA 22 Feb 2003

Arizona Lupine is a showy annual 4"–20" tall of sandy washes, in bloom Jan–May.

WEST COAST LADY
Vanessa annabella

Size: Medium (1¹/₂"–2")　　　　　　　　　　*Flies:* Jan–Dec (several flights)

West Coast Lady nectaring on Sand Verbena

All three Lady species look much alike. To tell them apart attention to pattern details is needed. The West Coast Lady's upperside is brighter orange than the Painted Lady's and has an orange bar rather than white near the black tip of the forewing; on the hindwing look for a row of blue eyespots.

Like other Ladies, the West Coast Lady can not stand freezing climates. As its name implies, it is only a permanent resident near the west coast of the U.S. and Baja. In our area it is not as common a butterfly as the Painted Lady.

In spring it sips several flowers—Sand Verbena in Borrego Valley, Desert Apricot in Box Canyon, Oakleaf Gooseberry in Culp Valley. Males perch to await females on hilltops such as Montezuma Vista Point.

West Coast Lady perched on Cheeseweed, a caterpillar food plant

Caterpillar Food Plants, Egg, Caterpillar and Chrysalis

MALLOW FAMILY: Cheeseweed, *Malva parviflora* (below left & p. 94); Apricot Mallow, *Sphaeralcea ambigua* (below top center & right & pp. 94, 95); NETTLE FAMILY: Hoary Nettle, *Urtica dioica* (p. 75).

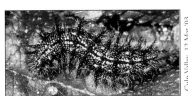

Caterpillar on Apricot Mallow

Below: *Egg on Cheeseweed*
Right: *Chrysalis*

Cheeseweed, a weedy annual 1'–3' tall, has lobed toothed leaves and small pinkish flowers any time.

Apricot Mallow, a woody perennial 20"–3' tall of canyons and rocky slopes has coral flowers Mar–Jul.

77

AMERICAN LADY
Vanessa virginiensis
Size: Med–Lge (1³/₄"–2¹/₂") *Flies:* Feb–Dec (sev flts)

Boulder Co, CO 11 Aug 2001

American Lady
Above:
upperside
Right:
underside

Boulder Co, CO 5 Jul 1999

Distinguish the American Lady, from the other two Ladies (pp. 76, 77) by the small white dot just below the black tip of the upperside forewing and the particularly pretty cobweb-like pattern with two large eyespots on the underside hindwing,

In our area this Lady, like the other two Ladies that cannot tolerate cold winters in any of its life stages, may live all year. Each spring it migrates to colonize other areas. Males perch for mates. Adults sip nectar.

CALIFORNIA TORTOISESHELL
Nymphalis californica
Size: Med (1³/₄"–2¹/₄") *Flies:* Jan–Nov (1 long flt)

Boulder Co, CO 11 Aug 2001

California Tortoiseshell
Above:
upperside
Right:
underside

Cuyamaca Rancho SP, CA 1 Jun '03

Not a resident here, this Tortoiseshell may reach our area during years of eruption when it migrates in huge numbers. Spring 2003 we saw several overwintering adults—at Culp Valley, hilltopping at Montezuma Vista Point, in the mountains.

Caterpillar Food Plant

BUCKTHORN FAMILY: Wedgeleaf Ceanothus, *Ceanothus cuneatus* (p. 45).

Caterpillar and its Food Plant

SUNFLOWER FAMILY: mainly Everlastings, *Gnaphalium* spp (below and right).

Borrego Springs, CA 16 May 1997

American Lady caterpillar on Everlasting, a rather spindly annual species to 1' tall. It is woolly with small pearly flowers in spring.

This Everlasting, another of several species in our area, grows 18"–30" tall in rocky moist canyons. It has pearly white flowers in spring.

Hellhole Canyon ABDSP, CA 13 Mar 2000

MOURNING CLOAK
Nymphalis antiopa

Size: Large   (2¹/₄"—3")   *Flies:* Jan–Dec (usually 1 long flight)

Mourning Cloak perching on Baccharis

Sentenac Cienega ABDSP, CA 12 Mar 1999

This large butterfly is unique and readily identified. The common name refers to its somber tone while the species name, Antiopa, leader of the Amazons in Greek mythology, suggests an impressive butterfly, which, indeed, it is.

It flies in riparian locales where cottonwoods and willows, the caterpillar food plants, grow —Borrego Palm, Hellhole, Bitter Creek Canyons, Sentenac Cienega. Look up above trees and taller shrubs to see it gliding by.

Mourning Cloaks sip flower nectar, fruit, sap and mud. Males perch on branches to wait for mates. This long-lived butterfly, perhaps up to a full year, emerges from the chrysalis in the summer and overwinters. Females mate in spring and lay eggs in bands encircling tree twigs. The hatched caterpillars remain in a group eating leaves until they finally wander off to transform into chrysalises in safe places.

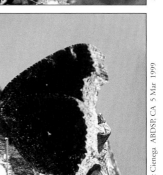

Sentenac Cienega ABDSP, CA 5 Mar 1999

Mourning Cloak, underside

Caterpillar Food Plants & Caterpillar

WILLOW FAMILY: Fremont Cottonwood, *Populus fremontii* (below left); Slender Willow, *Salix exigua* (pp. 44, 82).

Bitter Creek Canyon ABDSP, CA 9 Mar 2003

Bitter Creek Canyon ABDSP, CA 9 Mar 2003

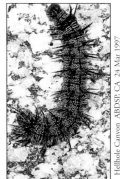

Hellhole Canyon ABDSP, CA 24 Mar 1997

Fremont Cottonwood is a deciduous tree that can grow to 90' in moist places. It is common along streams. This lone Fremont Cottonwood marks Bitter Creek Spring.

Fremont Cottonwood leaves are large, triangular and coarsely scalloped.

Mourning Cloak caterpillar on a boulder looking for a safe spot to form its chrysalis.

79

COMMON BUCKEYE
Junonia coenia

Size: Medium-Large (1⁵/₈"–2³/₈")   *Flies:* Jan–Dec (several flights)

Hellhole Canyon ABDSP, CA 15 Oct 1998

Common Buckeye perching on ground

The large peacock eyespots on a warm brown ground color makes the Buckeye, sometimes called the Peacock Butterfly, distinctive. These eyespots flashing in flight may scare away predacious birds.

The Buckeye is an all-year resident only in the milder climates along the west coast and southern U.S. border, moving northward as the season warms.

These butterflies visit flowers for nectar and drink at damp sand or mud. The Buckeye has a characteristic flight of gliding between wing flaps. Males patrol short distances back and forth in sunny open areas, perching frequently on bare ground, a favorite rock or low plants to wait for females.

Look for Buckeyes in most habitats from desert washes and canyons to mountain meadows and peaks.

Hellhole Canyon ABDSP 26 Mar 1996

Common Buckeye, underside

Caterpillar Food Plants

PLANTAIN FAMILY: Southwestern Plantain, *Plantago patagonica* (below left & p. 74). SNAP-DRAGON FAMILY: Purple Owl's-Clover, *Castilleja exserta* (below center); White Snapdragon, *Antirrhinum coulterianum* (below right).

Near Jacumba ABDSP, CA 25 Apr 2001

Near Scissors Crossing ABDSP, CA 2 May 1998

Culp Valley ABDSP, CA 23 Mar 1998

Southwestern Plantian, a tufted hairy annual 2"-8" tall, has cylindrical flower spikes and tiny flowers in Apr-Jun.

Purple Owl's-Clover is an annual 4"-16" high with white to purplish-red lobed bracts and flowers Mar-Jun.

White Snapdragon, an annual 1'-4' tall, grows among desert shrubs or on chaparral burns. White flowers bloom Mar-Jul.

COMMON RINGLET
Coenonympha tullia california
Size: Small (1¼"–1⅜")   *Flies:* Feb–Nov (sev flts)

Mission Dam SD Co, CA 24 Apr 2001

Common Ringlet perching

The Common Ringlet, like most other Satyrs in North America, is well camouflaged with earthtone colors. It can be readily identified from the underside (seen when perching) by the brownish–grayish color with a contrasting jagged cream band, the single eyespot on the forewing and the series of eyespots on the hindwing. The upperside is creamy.

Like woodland nymphs Ringlets fly close to the ground with an erratic skipping and dancing, often stopping to perch on the ground or low vegetation with wings closed. Their cryptic pattern makes them hard to see.

Ringlets do not live in deserts. Look for the Common Ringlet at higher elevations in the cooler, grassy habitats of chaparral, woodlands and grasslands. They may aestivate to avoid the hot summer.

The Ringlet, as with all Satyrs, has a short proboscis and prefers sap, animal droppings, rotting fruit and mud to flower nectar. Males patrol and perch to seek mates.

Caterpillar Food Plants

GRASS FAMILY: Kentucky Bluegrass, *Poa pratensis* (p. 101); Needlegrass, *Stipa* spp. (not shown).

GREAT BASIN WOOD-NYMPH
Cercyonis sthenele silvestris
Size: Sm–Med (1¼"–1¾")   *Flies:* May–Sep (1 flt)

Glendova, CA 11 Jul 1951 U of CO Museum

Great Basin Wood-Nymph female, underside

The Great Basin Wood-Nymph is recognized by the brown mottled pattern on the underside (visable when it sits) and by very few to no small spots on the hindwing. Seen on both the upper- and underside forewings are two large eyespots ringed with yellow. Usually the upper eyespot is larger than the lower one. Sometimes in females these two eyespots are close to the same size (see photo above).

Adults nectar at flowers. Males patrol all day for females. Look for this Wood-Nymph in open grassy oak woodlands and in chaparrel at elevations over 3500 ft along the western border of our area such as the Sunrise Highway and near Ranchita.

Caterpillar Food Plant

GRASS FAMILY: Grasses, probably Squirreltail, *Elymus elymoides,* just reported for *C. sthenele behrii,* the first California food plant recorded for this species, by Emmel & Pratt, 2003.

Squirreltail, aptly named, is an erect perennial grass 4"–26" tall with the "squirreltail" a vertical series of long awned spikelets, two at each node of the inflorescence.

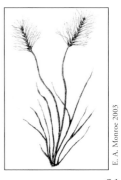

E. A. Monroe 2003

LORQUIN'S ADMIRAL
Limenitis lorquini

Size: Medium–Large (2"–2⁵/₈") *Flies:* Feb–Nov (2 flights)

Borrego Palm Canyon ABDSP, CA 12 Apr 1996

Lorquin's Admiral perched on Desert Fan Palm

Named after Pierre Lorquin, a Frenchman who discovered this and other species in the mid-1800s, Lorquin's is recognized by the black upperside with a bold white band and an orange patch elongated partway down the forewing margin.

Lorquin's flies by flapping, then gliding, frequently stopping to perch. Males seek mates in this way. It seldom sips flowers. Look for it in canyons with water and Willows, such as Borrego Palm, Hellhole, Oriflamme.

A recent study by Prudic *et al*, 2002 found this species mimics the very similar but distasteful Sister (opposite), thereby gaining protection from birds that have learned to avoid the Sister.

Borrego Palm Canyon ABDSP, CA 12 Apr 1996

Lorquin's Admiral, underside

Caterpillar Food Plants

WILLOW FAMILY: Arroyo Willow, *S. lasiolepis* (not shown); other Willows, *Salix* spp, probably including Slender Willow, *Salix exigua* (below left & p. 44) and Largeleaf Willow, *S. laevigata* (below right). Also, ROSE FAMILY: Western Chokecherry, *Prunus virginiana* (p. 23).

Borrego Palm Canyon ABDSP, CA 12 Apr 1996

Upper Oriflamme Can ABDSP, CA 21 May 1997

Lorquin's Admiral perching on Slender Willow, a common streamside shrub 6'–15' tall. Its very elongate leaves only ¹/₈" to ³/₈" wide are sometimes slightly toothed.

Lorquin's Admiral perching on a Large-leaf Willow, a tree 20'–50' tall that grows along streams and in canyons.

CALIFORNIA SISTER
Adelpha bredowii californica

Size: Large (2¼"–3")   *Flies:* Mar–Nov (2 flights)

California Sister perched on Oak Gooseberry

Culp Valley ABDSP, CA 3 May 1998

The name Sister may refer to the black and white coloration resembling a nun's garb. The Sister, looking like a Lorquin's big sister, has a large orange patch, black-bordered, *not* extending down the margin.

Sisters fly with a graceful, stately glide. They sip Yerba Santa and often drink at damp earth where one can approach them quite closely.

Males patrol and perch to find mates. We see the Sister near oaks, such as at Culp Valley and Upper Oriflamme Canyon.

Sisters, distasteful to birds, became models for the tasty Lorquin's that evolved as a mimic to gain protection from bird predators (Prudic *et al,* 2002).

California Sister, underside, perched on Sugarbush

Culp Valley ABDSP, CA 8 Apr 2001

Caterpillar Food Plants

OAK FAMILY: Canyon Live Oak, *Quercus chrysolepis* (below left & p. 43); California Black Oak, *Q. kelloggii* (below right); California Live Oak, *Q. agrifolia* (p. 91); Scrub Live Oak, *Q. wislizeni* var *frutescens* (p. 43).

Kwaaymii Point ABDSP, CA 26 Jun 2000

Sunrise Highway SD Co, CA 7 May 2001

Canyon Live Oak is an evergreen tree 20'–60' tall or shrub (var *nana*, above). New growth on twigs and leaf undersides has a fine golden fuzz that turns gray-felty, then smooth.

California Black Oak, a deciduous tree 30'–80' high, has lustrous green leaves with deep lobes that end in bristle-tipped teeth. Look for it at Kwaaymii Point and Garnet Peak.

83

MONARCH
Danaus plexippus

Size: Large (3¹/₄"–4")   *Flies:* Jan–Dec (several flights)

Borrego Springs, CA 13 Oct 1998

Monarch male. The two dark hindwing scent patches are non-functional

Imposing and familiar, the Monarch is famous for its annual migrations. In spring it leaves wintering sites along the California coast and in Mexico to fly northward. After several generations the last adults of the year are long-lived (up to 9 months) and return in the fall for communal overwintering by the millions. These same adults start the northern spring migration, mating en route to start the next life cycle.

Borrego Springs, CA 10 Oct 1998

Males patrol for mates. The pheromone (mating odor) patches on the male upperside hindwings are no longer used. The bright colors of caterpillars and adults are a warning to predators they are poisonous due to the milkweed chemicals eaten by the caterpillar.

Although not common here, look for them in all habitats as they fly by or visit flowers.

Monarch on Lantana

Caterpillar Food Plants, Egg, Caterpillars and Chrysalis

MILKWEED FAMILY: California Milkweed, *Asclepias californica* (below left); Desert Milkweed, *A. erosa* (below right).

Mt Palomar SD Co, CA 27 Jun 2000

Cima, CA 10 Oct 2003

Caterpillars on Desert Milkweed

Below: *Egg magnified 15 times*
Right: *Jade pupa*

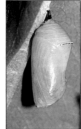

San Felipe Valley–BLM SD Co, CA 28 Jun 2000

California Milkweed, a woolly perennial 12"–22" high of dry slopes, has large leaves and purplish flowers Apr–Jul.

Desert Milkweed, a perennial 20"– 40" tall of dry slopes, has large leaves and whitish flowers May–Jul.

QUEEN
Danaus gilippus

Size: Large (2⅝"-3⅜")   *Flies:* Jan–Dec (several flights)

Queen male sipping Baccharis. Note the dark scent patches on the hindwings

Sentenac Cienega ABDSP, CA 12 Oct 2003

The Queen, similar to the Monarch, is a bit smaller and browner. Both are poisonous due to milkweed chemicals their caterpillars eat. Neither can stand cold winters in any life-cycle stage and so are year-long residents only in the extreme southern U.S. In summer both migrate northward over much of the U.S., but Queens lack the mass return.

Males patrol to find mates. The dark patches on the males upperside hindwings secrete a pheromone (mating odor) as an aid for mating. Adults take nectar from many kinds of flowers and sip damp soil.

Queens may fly anywhere.

Queen Near right: *male sipping Baccharis* Far right: *female sipping Alkali Goldenbush*

Sentenac Cienega ABDSP, CA 12 Oct 2003

Bow Willow ABDSP, CA 4 Nov 1995

Caterpillar Food Plants, Egg and Caterpillar

MILKWEED FAMILY: Smooth Milkvine, *Sarcostemma hirtellum* (below left top); Climbing Milkvine, *S. cynanchoides* ssp *hartwegii* (below left bottom); Rush Milkweed, *Asclepias subulata* (below center); White-stemmed Milkweed, *A. albicans* (below right); Desert Milkweed, *A. erosa* (p. 84).

Hellhole Can 30 Apr '00

Borrego Palm C 28 Feb '00

Visitor Center ABDSP, CA 3 May 2000

San Felipe Val–BLM SD Co, CA 20 Oct '03

Mountain Palm Springs ABDSP, CA 16 Mar 2000

Smooth Milkvine (top) blooms Apr–May & *Climbing Milkvine* (bottom) Feb–Jul.

Rush Milkweed, tall and wandlike with ephemeral leaves, blooms in sandy washes Apr-Dec .

Caterpillar on Desert Milkweed

White-stemmed Milkweed with egg has tall waxy stems, ephemeral leaves, flowers Mar-May.

85

Skippers (HESPERIIDAE)

Named for their darting, short flight and frequent perching, these small to medium-sized insects differ from other butterflies by their stout, hairy bodies, large heads and eyes. Most have the club at the end of the antennae bent back into a hook. They come in shades of brown, orange, gray, black and white. This large worldwide family is most abundant in the American tropics. Of the 276 species found in the U.S., 34 species occur in our area.

THREE SUBFAMILIES occur in Anza-Borrego Desert State Park® and environs.

SPREAD-WINGS (PYRGINAE): Sit with their wings spread wide open. (18 species)

GRASS SKIPPERS (HESPERIINAE): So named because their caterpillars eat mainly grasses. Males of most species have a dark patch of scent scales on their forewings called a stigma. They sit either with both wings closed, or with forewings partly open and hindwings wide open. (14 species)

GIANT-SKIPPERS (MEGATHYMINAE): These large skippers, unlike our other skippers, lack a hook on their antennal club, never feed at flowers and have small heads, narrower than the body. As indicated by their robust bodies, Giants fly extremely fast, but often return to the same spot to perch. They may sit with wings held in the same unique way as Grass Skippers. Most of the dozen or so species in the U.S. live in the arid southwest where their food plants grow. (2 species)

Mojave Sootywing
A SPREAD-WING SKIPPER

Orange Skipperling
A GRASS SKIPPER

California Giant-Skipper
A GIANT-SKIPPER

HABITS:
- The stout body is heavily muscled, giving them a faster flight than most other butterflies, a flight so rapid as to blur the wings.
- Most skippers have long proboscises. They sip moisture from damp sand or mud and feed on flower nectar and bird droppings. Female Giant-Skippers never eat.
- Males of most species perch awaiting females; a few, especially some Spread-wings, patrol.

PLANTS EATEN BY THE CATERPILLARS: In our area **SPREAD-WINGS** eat plants in the Amaranth, Buckthorn, Goosefoot, Mallow, Oak, Pea and Rose Families. **GRASS SKIPPERS** eat grasses and sedges. One of our **GIANT-SKIPPERS** eats agaves, the other yuccas.

Egg: Usually spherical with a broad, flattened base, laid singly on leaves.

Caterpillar (larva): Plain, smooth except for tiny hairs, sometimes with horns and tails. A large head joined to a narrow "neck" (except for Giant-Skippers) identifies them instantly as skippers. Most species silk together a leaf tube where they live and pupate protected from predators, emerging at night to feed.

Chrysalis (pupa): Caterpillars pupate in a cocoon made of leaves fastened together with silk. Chrysalises are simple in shape, some with a head horn or long proboscis.

Hibernation: Most skippers in our region over-winter as caterpillars.

ARIZONA POWDERED-SKIPPER
Systasea zampa

Size: Small (1"–1¹/₂")   *Flies:* Jan–Oct (several flights)

Arizona Powdered-Skipper sipping Fernleaf Phacelia

Culp Valley ABDSP, CA 23 Mar 1998

The uncommon Arizona Powdered Skipper is unique among our butterflies. With its soft colors and scalloped wings, it looks quite moth-like— except for the hooks on its clubbed antennae.

This handsome skipper flies in desert washes and canyons near rocky slopes where its caterpillar food plants, Rock Hibiscus and Yellow Feltplant, grow. Look for it in Hellhole Canyon, Culp Valley and the Scissors Crossing area.

Powdered-Skippers sip mud or moist sand and nectar at flowers including Fernleaf Phacelia and Desert Lavender. Males perch to await females, often near or on nectar plants.

Near Scissors Crossing ABDSP, CA 2 May 1998

Arizona Powdered-Skipper, underside

Caterpillar Food Plants

MALLOW FAMILY: Yellow Feltplant, *Horsfordia newberryi* (below left); Rock Hibiscus, *Hibiscus denudatus* (below right & p. 48); Palmer Abutilon, *Abutilon palmeri* (not shown).

Hellhole Can 18 Mar 2003   *Insert:* Hellhole 23 Apr '91

Near Hellhole Canyon ABDSP, CA 16 Mar 2001

Yellow Feltplant, an erect slightly branched subshrub 3'–8' tall of desert rocky slopes has heavily felted yellow green leaves and small-ish yellow flowers Mar–Apr & Nov–Dec.

Rock Hibiscus, a subshrub 1'–2' tall of desert washes, bajadas and rocky slopes has toothed oval matted wooly leaves and showy whitish to pink-lavender flowers Mar–May & Nov–Dec.

87

NORTHERN CLOUDYWING
Thorybes pylades
Size: Sm–Med (1¹/₄"–1⁷/₈") *Flies:* Mar–Jul (1 flt)

Northern Cloudywing on Manzanita

The Northern Cloudywing flies in our higher montains. Our favorite place to see it is Garnet Peak where males perch on shrubs such as Manzanita and Cupleaf Ceanothus near the hilltop to await mates. It takes nectar from Ceanothus and an array of other flowers and also visits mud.

It sits with wings half open to show the dark brown upperside with brown checkered fringe and a few glassy white spots. Two short rows of clear white spots near the front margin of the wing help identify it.

Caterpillar Food Plant
PEA FAMILY: False Indigo, *Amorpha fruticosa* (below & p. 34); other peas.

False indigo, flower detail. This deciduous shrub 3'–6' tall has long wands of tiny flowers with only one petal, the purple banner, and ten protruding stamens Mar–Jul.

SLEEPY DUSKYWING
Erynnis brizo lacustra
Size: Sm–Med (1¹/₄"–1⁵/₈") *Flies:* Mar–Jul (1 flt)

Sleepy Duskywing sipping Desert Apricot

Erynnis, the genus name of these dark Duskywings, means, aptly, an evening spirit. Brizo, the species name, means sleep.

The Sleepy Duskywing often sits with wings open showing its forewings with a well-defined pattern of dark crossbands and *no* apical white spots and its brown hindwings.

In early spring males hilltop for mates at Montezuma Vista or Kwaaymii Points. In Lower Oriflamme Canyon, Culp Valley and Banner it sips mud and visits flowers—Fernleaf Phacelia, Desert Apricot, Mulefat.

Caterpillar Food Plant
OAK FAMILY: Desert Scrub Oak, *Quercus cornelius- mulleri* (below).

The Desert Scrub Oak with small evergreen leaves, spiny or entire, dull green on the upper surface, finely white-felted below, grows 3'–8' tall on rocky slopes.

PACUVIUS DUSKYWING
Erynnis pacuvius callidus
Size: Sm (1¹/₄"–1³/₈") *Flies:* Mar–Oct (2 flights)

Pacuvius Duskywing, mating pair

Pacuvius is hard to tell in the field from some other Duskywing species. (All Duskywings are a challenge to tell apart.) The upperside forewing is mottled gray-brown with irregular darker patches. Look for a row of tiny glassy white spots near the apex. The hindwing is brown with brown fringe.

Pacuvius flies in chaparral and in the mountains, visiting flowers and mud, but is not commonly seen. Males perch on hilltops such as Garnet Peak as a rendezvous site awaiting females to fly up.

Caterpillar Food Plants

BUCKTHORN FAMILY: Probably Cupleaf Ceanothus, *Ceanothus greggii* (below); Hairy Ceanothus, *C. oliganthus* (not shown).

Cupleaf Ceanothus, a chaparral shrub 2'–6' tall, has distinctive thick toothed blunt-tipped leaves which are cup-shaped and clusters of white flowers Mar–Jul.

AFRANIUS DUSKYWING
Erynnis afranius
Size: Sm (1¹/₈"–1³/₈") *Flies:* Feb–Aug (2 flights)

Afranius Duskywing sipping moist sand

Like other Duskywings, Afranius is dark and usually sits with wings open, showing its upperside. The forewing is mottled gray-black with a few white dots and often a patch of brown near the wingtip. The hindwing is plain brown-black with a row of pale spots and the fringe is brown-tan.

Afranius nectars at flowers and sips damp soil. Males do not hilltop, but perch in canyons and gulches to wait for mates.

Look for it from the Scissors Crossing/San Felipe region to the Laguna Meadows.

Caterpillar Food Plants

PEA FAMILY: Nevada Lotus, *Lotus nevadensis* (below); Spanish Clover, *Lotus purshianus* (p. 60).

Nevada Lotus is a prostrate perennial which forms a mat 12"–30" wide, growing on dry slopes above 3500'. It has pinnate leaves and yellow often red-tinged flowers May–Aug.

89

FUNEREAL DUSKYWING
Erynnis funeralis

SIze: Small–Medium (1³/₈"–1³/₄")   *Flies:* Jan–Nov (several flights)

Yaqui Well ABDSP, CA 10 Mar 2000

Funereal Duskywing nectaring on Bladderpod

Named for its somber color, this early spring to fall flier is our most common and wide-ranging Duskywing. We see it from desert washes and canyons to mountains, but especially in hot, dry places.

Funereal is easily confused with the Mournful Duskywing (opposite), since both Duskywings have a distinctive white

Upper Oriflamme Canyon ABDSP, CA 21 May 1997

hindwing fringe. Distinguish these two look-alikes by Funereal's narrower forewings, the pale brown upperside forewing patch near the wingtip and the double row of obscure white dots along the margin of the underside hindwing. Also, Funereal flies in a wide range of habitats whereas Mournful may be expected in chaparral and oak woodlands.

Males perch on shrubs at eye level, periodically taking short flights. Adults sip nectar from many flowers—Desert Apricot, Desert Lavender, Bladderpod, Fiddleneck, Catclaw, Sugarbush and Butterweed.

Funereal Duskywings, mating pair

Caterpillar Food Plants

PEA FAMILY: Desert Ironwood, *Olneya tesota* (below); Deerweed, *Lotus scoparius* (pp. 48, 57, 59); several other peas.

Box Canyon Mecca, CA 23 May 1990

Box Canyon Mecca, CA 28 Apr 2000

Desert Ironwood is a grayish tree about 16'–26' tall with a broad crown and scaly bark. Its hard dense wood is used for carvings by the Seri Indians. It grows in desert washes.

Desert Ironwood has short racemes of pale rosy-purple pea-like flowers that bloom Apr–May and grayish pinnate leaves. Pods are thick and narrowed between seeds.

MOURNFUL DUSKYWING
Erynnis tristis
Size: Sm–Med (1¼"–1⅝") *Flies:* Jan–Nov (sev flts)

Mournful Duskywing nectaring on Narrowleaf Goldenbush

Mournful and Funereal (opposite) are the only Duskywings here with a white hind-wing fringe. Mournful's upperside forewing is brown-black with dark markings and a few glassy white spots. The hindwing is plain brown with or without a row of indistinct white spots along the under hindwing margin.

Males perch on shrubs on hilltops such as Montezuma Vista Point and Garnet Peak waiting for females. We see adults sip Narrowleaf Goldenbush and Sunflower.

Caterpillar Food Plants

OAK FAMILY: California Live Oak, *Quercus agrifolia* (below left, right); Scrub Live Oak, *Q. wizlizeni* (p. 43); probably Desert Scrub Oak, *Q. cornelius-mulleri* (p. 88).

California Live Oak is a majestic evergreen oak with smooth bark and a wide crown which grows up to 80' high in valleys and on slopes in chaparral and oak woodlands.

PROPERTIUS DUSKYWING
Erynnis propertius
Size: Sm–Med (1⅜"–1¾") *Flies:* Feb–Sep (1 flt)

Propertius Duskywing

Like other Duskywings, Propertius sits with open wings to show the upperside. The forewing is brown-gray with black markings and glassy spots while the hindwing is lighter brown with pale spots and brown fringe.

Adults sip mud and flowers—Cryptantha, Desert Apricot, Mulefat, Buckwheat. Males perch on hilltops to await mates. Look for this spring flier in desert transition, chaparral and oak woodlands—Culp Valley, Banner Grade, Lower Oriflamme Canyon.

Caterpillar Food Plant

OAK FAMILY: California Live Oak, *Quercus agrifolia* (below left, right); probably other oaks.

California Live Oak leaves are leathery and strongly convex on the upper side. In ssp. *oxyadenia* (above) leaf undersides have dense star-shaped hairs. Acorns are slender, pointed.

91

MOJAVE SOOTYWING
Hesperopsis libya

Size: Small (1"–1¹/₈")   *Flies:* Mar–Oct (2–3 flights)

Mojave Sootywing female nectaring at Desert Arrowweed

The Mojave Sootywing is is our only dark skipper living in the low desert with white spots above and below and a pale but not white fringe. Look for it along desert washes and in alkaline flats flying around saltbush, the caterpillar food, and nectaring on nearby flowers. When you see one there is apt to be a small colony nearby.

One location to find the Mojave is west of the Borrego Springs dump in the Honey Mesquite hummock dunes where males patrol around saltbush and both sexes sip Honey Mesquite or Stephanomeria. Also look for it at in alkaline saltbush habitats—at Yaqui Well visiting Alkali Goldenbush or the Borrego Sink sipping Desert Arrowweed, Sandpaper Plant or Jackass-Clover.

Mojave Sootywing male sipping Desert Arrowweed

Mojave Sootywing male sipping Sandpaper Plant

Caterpillar Food Plant

GOOSEFOOT FAMILY: Four-winged Saltbush, *Atriplex canescens* (below)

Four-winged Saltbush is a common shrub 18"– 5' high that thrives on sandy flats, washes and alkali areas. Male and female flowers, borne on different plants Jun–Aug, are wind-pollinated.

Each seed of Four-winged Saltbush has four wings. The many leaves, attached directly to the stem at their bases, are linear.

92

COMMON SOOTYWING
Pholisora catullus

Size: Tiny (⅞"–1")   *Flies:* Mar–Nov (2–3 flights)

Common Sootywing nectaring on Narrowleaf Goldenbush

This little Sootywing can be identified by the glossy, sooty-black or dark brown color of the wings. Forewings have a pattern of white spots on the outer portion of the wings on both the upper- and under-sides; hindwings have only one row of tiny whitish spots along the margin on the upperside, but are solid black on the underside. Some white dots even occur on top of the black head.

Look for this shiny black Sootywing found sparingly in desert transition zones where chaparral and desert meet. We see it occasionally in spring or fall at Culp Valley and the San Felipe Valley-BLM area sipping moist mud or sand or sipping flowers such as Narrowleaf Goldenbush or Buckwheat. Males patrol just above the ground seeking females.

Common Sootywing , underside with dots on forewing and unmarked hindwing, at moist sand

Caterpillar Food Plants

AMARANTH FAMILY: Amaranths such as Fringe Amaranth, *Amaranthus fimbriatus* (below left). GOOSEFOOT FAMILY: California Goosefoot, *Chenopodium californicum* (below center); White Pigweed, *C. murale* (below right).

Fringe Amaranth, an erect annual 16"–40" tall, has clusters of tiny fringed flowers arranged in spikes Aug–Nov.

California Goosefoot, a perennial 12"–32" tall with triangular toothed leaves, has dense terminal flower spikes Mar–Jun.

White Pigweed, a branched annual (native to Europe), has "goosefoot" leaves and tiny flowers Jan–Dec.

93

WHITE CHECKERED-SKIPPER
Pyrgus albescens

Size: Small (1"–1¼") *Flies:* Jan–Dec (several flights)

White Checkered-Skipper on Cinchweed

The White Checkered-Skipper flits along rapidly and low to the ground, stopping to sip wet soil or flowers.

Male uppersides are grayish brown-black with bands of white spots; the body and wing bases may have bluish gray hairs. Females are darker. Wing fringes are white with black checkers that extend the full width of the fringe. The underside hindwing is white with two irregular brownish bands bordered with fine black lines.

Males patrol to and fro over a patch of dry wash or trail, perching often on bare ground. Adults sip many flowers—Cryptantha, Spanish Needles, Tidytips, Wild Heliotrope, Cinchweed Sand Verbena. Common and widespread, it flies in our hot deserts and also at higher elevations, wherever the mallows its caterpillars eat are found.

White Checkered-Skipper sipping Wild Heliotrope

Caterpillar Food Plants

MALLOW FAMILY: Cheeseweed, *Malva parviflora* (below left & p. 77); Apricot Mallow, *Sphaeralcea ambigua* (below right & pp. 77, 95); Desert Fivespot, *Eremalche rotundifolia* (p. 96).

Cheeseweed, a native of Eurasia, is a tallish weedy annual with small pinkish flowers that grows in disturbed places, including along some roadsides in Borrego Springs.

Apricot Mallow is a perennial shrub to 3' tall with many erect or spreading stems from the base. Its twisted buds unfurl to graceful grenadine flowers Mar-Jul.

SMALL CHECKERED-SKIPPER
Pyrgus scriptura
Size: Tiny (³/₄"–1")   *Flies:* Feb–Nov (sev flts)

Small Checkered–Skipper
Above: **upperside**
Right: **underside**

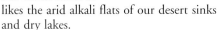

This tiny checkered butterfly occurs sparingly in our desert areas. It likes the arid alkali flats of our desert sinks and dry lakes.

Identification is made by its small size, the brownish black coloration with small white spots on the upperside and with a white spot in the center of the hindwing. The underside hindwing is pale brown with indistinct white spots. Wing fringes are white with some dark checks extending only part way.

Look for males patrolling close to the ground or sometimes perching on the ground awaiting females. Adults feed on flower nectar, mud and dung.

Caterpillar Food Plant

MALLOW FAMILY: Apricot Mallow, *Sphaeralcea ambigua* (below & pp. 77 & 94).

The beautiful Apricot Mallow flower. This Mallow of rocky hillsides and washes has wavy-edged leaves with star-shaped hairs.

'LAGUNA' TWO-BANDED CHECKERED-SKIPPER   *Pyrgus ruralis lagunae*
Size: Small (~1")   *Flies:* Apr–Jul (1 flight)

'Laguna' Two-banded Checkered–Skipper
Above: **upperside**
Right: **underside**

Unlike the White Checkered-Skipper (opposite page), this checkered skipper is rare indeed, being federally listed as endangered. An isolated population flies in a small protected moist meadow in the Laguna Mountains where its food plant grows.

The upperside is grayish to brownish with two white spot bands forming a crude X. The underside is pale tan-brown with white spots, resulting in a low contrast pattern characteristic of this subspecies. Wing fringes are a snappy black and white.

Low-flying, males patrol and sometimes perch to seek mates.

Caterpillar Food Plant

ROSE FAMILY: Cleveland's Horkelia, *Horkelia clevelandii* (below)

Cleveland's Horkelia, a clumped perennial of moist mountain meadows, has toothed pinnate leaves and small white flowers Jun–Aug.

95

NORTHERN WHITE-SKIPPER
Heliopetes ericetorum

Size: Small (1¼"–1⅜")   *Flies:* Feb–Nov (2 flights)

Hellhole Canyon ABDSP, CA 5 May 1998

Northern White-Skipper male nectaring on Trixis

This white skipper is a pleasant contrast to all the look-alike dark skippers. The male upperside is white with black chevrons along the wing borders. The female has more extensive dark markings. The underside is white with irregular tan stripes.

Northern White–Skippers fly in desert to foothill canyons and at higher elevations in chaparral and open woodland habitats. Males patrol for mates.

Adults sip damp sand and many flowers including Trixis, Buckwheat, Yerba Mansa, Alkali Goldenbush, Shrub Globemallow.

Look for them in Hellhole, Borrego Palm and Grapevine Canyons, Culp Valley, Sentenac Cienega, Garnet Peak Trail.

Quite similar to the female Northern is **Erichson's White-Skipper** (p. 105), a rare stray.

Borrego Palm Can ABDSP, CA 5 May '00

Culp Valley ABDSP, CA 18 Oct 2003

Two Northern White-Skipper males puddling at streamside

Northern White-Skipper female on bud of Shrub Globemallow

Caterpillar Food Plants

MALLOW FAMILY: Desert Fivespot, *Eremalche rotundifolia* (below left); probably Shrub Globemallow, *Malacothamnus densiflorus* (below right); Rock Hibiscus, *Hibiscus denudatus* (pp. 48, 87); Apricot Mallow, *Sphaeralcea ambigua* (pp. 77, 94, 95).

Borrego Springs, CA 16 Apr 1991

Culp Valley ABDSP, CA 18 Oct 2003

Shrub Globemallow is a shrub 3'–6 ' tall with hairy toothed leaves, often lobed. Clusters of rose-pink flowers arranged in tiers around a spike bloom Apr-Jul (and sometimes in the fall).

Desert Fivespot, an annual 4"–16" high of sandy desert washes, has roundish scalloped leaves. Globular flowers with five rosy to lilac petals with a carmine spot bloom Mar–May.

EUFALA SKIPPER
Lerodea eufala
Size: Small (1"–1¹/₄")   *Flies:* Feb–Dec (sev flts)

Sentenac Cienega ABDSP, CA 12 Oct 2003

Borrego Sink 20 Feb 2003

Eufala Skipper
Above: *perched on Yerba Mansa*
Right: *sipping Desert Arrowweed*

The Eufala Skipper flies in early spring—at the Borrego Sink sipping Desert Arrowweed or perching on cattails at the Visitor Center Pupfish Pool or nectaring at flowers along roadsides in Borrego Springs. We also see it in the fall at Sentenac Cienega visiting Wild Heliotrope. Males perch awaiting mates.

Identify it by the overall gray to brown color. The underside hindwing is ash gray with very faint spots. The upperside is grayish brown with a few small glassy white spots. Males lack the black stigma patch.

Caterpillar Food Plant

GRASS FAMILY: Bermuda Grass, *Cynodon dactylon* (below left, right).

Borrego Palm Can ABDSP 30 Apr 2001

Bermuda Grass at base of California Fan Palm. This creeping perennial grass of warm regions, native to Africa, grows in disturbed areas and sometimes is planted for lawns.

SACHEM
Atalopedes campestris
Size: Sm (1¹/₄"–1³/₈")   *Flies:* Mar–Oct (sev flts)

Oriflamme Canyon ABDSP 6 May 2000

Guadaloupe SP, TX

Sachem
Above: *male perching.*
Right: *female sipping Sunflower*

Sachem is also called the Field Skipper since it flies in fields, meadows and disturbed lands where Bermuda and Kentucky Bluegrass, its caterpillar food plants, grow. Adults sip flower nectar and males perch on vegetation or the ground to wait for mates. Look for it at Culp Valley or Oriflamme Canyon.

Identify males by a large, squarish black stigma on an orange upperside forewing with dark borders. Females have two large glassy spots and a black patch. The underside hindwing band of dull spots is more obvious on the brown female wing, than the gold male.

Caterpillar Food Plants

GRASS FAMILY: Bermuda Grass, *Cynodon dactylon* (below left, right); Kentucky Bluegrass, *Poa pratensis* (p. 101).

Borrego Springs, CA 19 Feb 2000

Bermuda Grass, growing by rhizomes, has erect stems 4"-16" high tipped with slender digit-like spikes, sometimes purplish in hue.

97

JUBA SKIPPER
Hesperia juba
Size: Sm-Med (1¼"–1⅝") *Flies:* Mar–Oct (2 flts)

Sentenac Cienega ABDSP 11 Oct 1998

Juba Skipper
Above: *nectaring on Alkali Goldenbush*
Right: *sipping sand*

Culp Valley 3 May 1998

Juba means mane in Latin, referring to hairlike scales on the body, a trait not unique to this skipper.

Recognize Juba by the underside of dull greenish brown with a bold array of large squarish white spots and the orange upperside with a vivid dark brown jagged border.

Juba flies at many locales—Sentenac and Box Canyons, Sentenac Cienega, Culp and San Felipe Valleys, Laguna Meadows, Garnet Peak. It sips damp soil or nectars at Parish Viguiera, Wild Onion, San Diego Sunflower, and Alkali, Narrowleaf and Wedgeleaf Goldenbushes. Males perch for mates.

WESTERN BRANDED SKIPPER
Hesperia colorado leussleri (= *comma l.*)
Size: Small (1⅛"–1¼")   *Flies:* May–Aug (1 flt)

Stephenson Peak SD Co, CA 26 May 2003

Western Branded Skipper Above: *on Cryptantha* Right: *sipping Mariposa*

Garnet Peak 20 May 1997

This skipper is named for the elongated black patch of scent scales on the upper forewing called a stigma or "brand." (Males of most species in the Grass Skipper Subfamily have this stigma.)

The yellowish brown under hindwing has a band of dull white or yellowish spots. The upperside, also yellowish brown, has dark borders and a rather pointed forewing.

We see this skipper from desert transition to montane, at Culp Valley, Oriflamme Canyon and Garnet and Stephenson Peaks, sipping wet soil and Mariposa Lilies, Sunflowers, Thistles. Males perch awaiting females.

Caterpillar Food Plants

GRASS FAMILY: Red Brome, *Bromus madritensis* ssp *rubens* (below); Kentucky Blue Grass, *Poa pratensis* (p. 101).

Borrego Springs, CA 20 Feb 2003

Red Brome, an annual exotic grass (native of Europe), has distinctive erect reddish panicles 1"–3" long which blooms Feb–Jun. It grows in open, disturbed places.

Caterpillar Food Plant

GRASS FAMILY: probably Tufted Fescue, *Vulpia octoflora* var *hirtella* (below).

Tufted Fescue, a tufted annual grass 2"–16" tall of burns, dry open areas and rocky slopes, has flattened, fan-like hairy spiklets and flowers Apr–Jun.

E A Monroe 2002

98

COLUMBIA SKIPPER
Hesperia columbia
Size: Small (1¹/₈"–1³/₈") *Flies:* Mar–Oct (2 flts)

Poser Mt SD Co, CA 7 May '67 SDNHM

Columbia Skipper
Above: *underside*
Right: *upperside*

Poser Mt SDNHM

The Columbia Skipper flies in chaparral—Upper Oriflamme Canyon and the Garnet and Combs Peak areas. Although it also flies in early spring, it is more commonly seen nectaring on Cudweed Aster in late summer to early fall.

The spot band on the yellowish brown under hindwing is short and uncurved with bright, silvery white spots. The upperside is bright tawny-orange with dark, deeply toothed borders and dark wing bases.

Males perch on hilltops to await females.

Caterpillar Food Plant

GRASS FAMILY: Junegrass, *Koeleria macrantha* (below).

Junegrass,
a perennial bunchgrass 8"–30" tall with basal leaves, grows on dry slopes. Each stem is topped by a narrow inflorescence in bloom May–Jun.

Boulder Co, CO 14 Jun 2002

LINDSEY'S SKIPPER
Hesperia lindseyi
Size: Small (1¹/₈"–1³/₈") *Flies:* May–Aug (1 flt)

LA Co, CA 1 Jun 1980 SDNHM

Lindsey's Skipper
Above: *underside*
Right: *upperside*

LA Co, CA SDNHM

Lindsey's Skipper so far has been found only in the most northern section of our area, in Riverside County. Usually it flies in grassy clearings in chaparral or oak woodlands.

This skipper is yellowish greenish brown on the underside hindwing with angular spots (creamy to yellow in males, whitish in females) that extend along the veins. On the upperside it is mainly orangish. Males have a black stigma.

Some Lindsey females lay their eggs on lichens. The tiny hatched caterpillars must then find their way from lichen to grasses.

Caterpillar Food Plant

GRASS FAMILY: California Oatgrass, *Danthonia californica* (below).

Oatgrass, a perennial bunchgrass 4"–40" tall growing in moist open areas, has basal and stem leaves and 1 to 5 spikelets on the inflorescence blooming May–Jul.

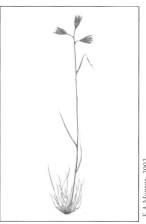

E A Monroe 2002

ORANGE SKIPPERLING
Copaeodes aurantiacus
Size: Tiny (³/₄"–1")   *Flies:* Feb–Nov (sev flts)

Orange Skipperling sipping Parish Viguiera

Orange Skipperling displaying dark wing bases and dark line around wing margins

True to its scientific name *aurantiacus*, Latin for gold color, this skipper is practically a pure golden orange. Though common in our area, it is small, flies rapidly and so is easy to overlook.

Identifying traits besides the overall golden orange (bright on the upperside, paler on the underside) are the tiny size, a black line around wing margins, dark upperside wing bases and white on the head and on the underside of the long abdomen.

Fond of hot canyons, washes and edges of chaparral, it nectars at flowers such as Fernleaf Phacelia, Everlasting, Desert Arrowweed and Sunflower. Males perch on flowers and low twigs to await mates and seem to protect a small area by darting off and then returning again. Look for it in Borrego Palm, Hellhole, Sentenac and Upper Tubb Canyons as well as higher elevations.

Caterpillar Food Plant
GRASS FAMILY: Bermuda Grass, *Cynodon dactylon* (p. 97)

ALKALI SKIPPER
Pseudocopaeodes eunus
Size: Small (1"–1¹/₄")   *Flies:* Apr–Oct (sev flts)

Alkali Skipper
Above: **underside with two whitish streaks**
Right: **bright orange upperside with black border and vein ends**

As the name Alkali Skipper implies, this rare skipper flies in desert habitats with salty alkaline soils where its caterpillar plant, Desert Saltgrass, grows. Likely locales to search for it are the Scissors Crossing/ San Felipe area, Sentenac Cienega, Yaqui Well and other alkaline desert seeps.

Identifying traits are the pale orange underside crossed by two lighter rays and the brighter orange upperside with the vein ends becoming black near the narrow black border.

Caterpillar Food Plant
GRASS FAMILY: Desert Saltgrass, *Distichlis spicata* var *stricta* (below & p. 101).

Desert Saltgrass is a creeping perennial grass 4"–20" tall with stiff leaves. It grows in moist alkali areas in desert/ desert transition habitats such as Yaqui Well and Sentenac Cienega.

SANDHILL SKIPPER
Polites sabuleti
Size: Tiny–Sm (⅞"–1¼") *Flies:* Feb–Nov (sev flts)

Sentenac Cienega ABDSP 11 Oct 1998

Sentenac Cienega 4 May '98

Sandhill Skipper
Above: *nectaring on*
Alkali Goldenbush
Right: *on Saltbush*

Despite its common name of Sandhill, the best habitat for seeing this skipper in our region is at alkaline soil locales where Saltgrass grows such as Yaqui Well and Sentenac Cienega. You may see it nectaring at Alkali Goldenbush in the fall. Males often perch on Saltgrass or low shrubs waiting for females.

Identify the Sandhill Skipper by the tan-brown underside hindwing with a band of connected yellowish spots and with yellowish veins ending in dark points at the wing margins. The orange upside has dark brown deeply-toothed wing borders.

Caterpillar Food Plant

GRASS FAMILY: Desert Saltgrass, *Distichlis spicata* var *stricta* (below & p. 100)

Yaqui Well ABDSP, CA 10 Mar 2000

Desert Saltgrass bears flattened spikelets of male flowers (taller than leaf blades) and female flowers (shorter than blades) on separate plants. They bloom Mar–Aug.

FIERY SKIPPER
Hylephila phyleus
Size: Sm (1⅛"–1⅜") *Flies:* Jan–Dec (sev flts)

Mission Gorge SD Co. CA 22 Jun 2000

Borrego Spgs 16 Mar 1999

Fiery Skipper Above:
mating pair (male at
right) Right: *female*
sipping Sand Verbena

Look for this skipper from the comfort of your veranda. Attracted to garden flowers, it is quite fond of Lantana in our Borrego Springs yard.

The Fiery prefers disturbed areas with weedy grasses such as along roadsides in Borrego Springs where they sip Sand Verbena and males perch for mates.

Identify the Fiery by the underside hindwing of yellow (male) or brownish-yellow (female) with scattered dark dots and the fiery orange-yellow upside with dark jagged wing borders. Also notice the very short antennae.

Caterpillar Food Plants

GRASS FAMILY: Kentucky Bluegrass, *Poa pratensis* (below); Bermuda Grass, *Cynodon dactylon* (pp. 97).

Boulder Co. CO 14 Jun 2002

Kentucky Bluegrass, a perennial of moist meadows that spreads by rhizomes, has stems 8"–28" high, boat-like leaf tips and a tall panicle-like inflorescence.

101

Rural Skipper
Ochlodes agricola
Size: Tiny-Small (⁷/₈"–1")   *Flies:* Mar–Jul (1 flt)

Garnet Peak SD Co, CA 26 Jun 2000

Rural Skippers nectaring at Sunflower
Above: *underside*
Right: *Rural Skipper female, upperside, with glassy spots on the forewing*

Garnet Peak 26 Jun 2000

The Rural Skipper is very similar to the Woodland Skipper (right). However, they are not often found together since the Rural flies March–July, earlier than the Woodland that commonly flies in late summer/fall.

The underside hindwing of the Rural Skipper has a band of yellowish spots, indistinct or absent, on the tawny orange-yellow (male) to pinkish brown (female) ground color. Both the Rural and the Woodland are small and yellow-orange on the upperside with dark brown wing borders and markings. Distinguishing features are the small glassy white spots on the upperside forewings (absent in the Woodland Skipper), both near the wingtip and around the male stigma and the corresponding female dark patch.

Look for the Rural in early to mid summer in fields and other grassy places. Agricola, its Latin scientific name, means "field dweller" (agri=field; cola=dwell). We see it along trails and open areas in chaparral such as at Garnet Peak, visiting sunflowers for their nectar as well as for convenient perches for males awaiting females.

Caterpillar Food Plant

GRASS FAMILY: Grasses. Particular species are not known.

Woodland Skipper
Ochlodes sylvanoides
Size: Tiny-Sm (⁷/₈"–1¹/₈")   *Flies:* May–Oct (1 flt)

Garnet Peak SD Co, CA 12 Oct 1998

Woodland Skipper
Above: *female underside* Right:
male taking off, displaying his stigma, a black elongate mark, on his forewing

Garnet Pk Trail 13 Oct 2003

The Woodland Skipper is mainly a late season butterfly, usually flying July to October. Across the west it is a common and adaptable butterfly. In our area it flies in chaparral openings and montane grassy areas, often in dappled sunshine. It is named from the Latin sylvanoid, meaning "of the woods."

Identify the Woodland by the uniform yellow-brown under hindwing with a more or less distinct band of light spots. The upperside is orange with brown borders, but has no glassy spots as in the similar Rural Skipper. The upperside forewing in males has a black stigma of specialized scent scales (see photo above) and a dusky patch between stigma and wingtip. In females there is a dark patch where the stigma of the male would be.

Woodland Skippers are fond of flowers, especially late-season asters and Saw-toothed Goldenbush, and they sip mud. Males perch to await mates, often on dried flower heads.

Look for them at higher elevations such as Kwaaymii Point and Garnet Peak.

Caterpillar Food Plants

GRASS FAMILY: Bermuda Grass, *Cynodon dactylon* (p. 97).

California Giant-Skipper
Agathymus stephensi

Size: Medium (2"–2¹/₄")   *Flies:* Sep–Oct (1 flight)

California Giant-Skipper perched on Desert Agave

The California Giant-Skipper has a very restricted range, living only in our desert region of California and northern Baja where Desert Agave, the caterpillar food plant grows.

Giant-Skippers, larger than other skippers, have a moth-like appearance with their fat bodies and small heads. Unlike other skippers, Giant-Skippers lack hooks on their antennal clubs.

The California Giant-Skipper flies only in the fall. Since our other Giant-Skipper, the Yucca Giant-Skipper (p. 104), flies only in the spring, they can not be confused.

Their flight is swift and hard to follow, but they often return to the same place, landing with head upward. Look for them in habitats rich in Agave such as Box, Sentenac and Plum Canyons, especially in early morning as they perch on canyon walls bathed in sunshine. Or on agaves or nearby shrubs where males perch awaiting females. Or in Borrego Palm or Hellhole Canyons where we see males sip moist sand. Neither sex visits flowers.

California Giant-Skipper on Desert Agave

Caterpillar Food Plant and Caterpillar
LILY FAMILY: Desert Agave, *Agave deserti* (below & right).

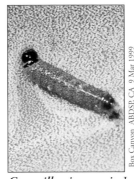

Desert Agave has handsome dense clusters of yellow flowers that bloom Mar–Jul, followed by distinctive brown seed pods.

Caterpillar in transit. It is rarely seen, for youngest larvae live inside the leaf tip, older inside the leaf base.

Desert Agave has a rosette of thick fibrous leaves with pale prickles tipped with a spine. The flower stalk is a magnificent 7'–16' tall.

103

YUCCA GIANT-SKIPPER
Megathymus yuccae harbisoni

Size: Medium–Large (2¹/₈"–2⁵/₈")   *Flies:* Mar–Apr (1 flight)

Cajun Pass LA Co, CA 15 Feb 1935 SDNHM

Yucca Giant-Skipper

The Yucca Giant-Skipper caterpiller eats Mojave Yucca, widespread in our area, but the butterfly is not often seen. It flies only in the spring. The newly-described sub-species *harbisoni*, first found one mile west of Scissors Crossing, differs from other sub-species such as *martini* pictured here (left) by having smaller spots and so appears darker.

Males perch near Yuccas in early morning. Adults are very fast fliers. Only males sip mud. Neither sex visits flowers.

Caterpillar Food Plant

LILY FAMILY: Mojave Yucca, *Yucca schidigera*, (right).

Mojave Yucca, a striking desert to chaparral tree-like lily 3'-15' tall, has a trunk and sharp daggerlike leaves, often with fibers separating from them. The stately panicles of large pendant creamy flowers often tinged with purple rise out of the center of the leaves Mar-May.

San Felipe Valley-BLM SD Co, CA 21 Mar 2000

Migrant & Stray Butterflies

These additional sixteen butterflies normally reside in areas outside of our region, but have wandered into our area at least once, some of them many times. Some of these butterfly species do not have caterpillar food plants here. Often these strays occur in years of bountiful rainfall, especially during the second year of a wet cycle. Seeing any one of these butterflies is a happy accident–but you may be lucky!

These butterfly sightings are based on records, both published and unpublished, by knowledgeable observers and on butterfly specimens in the San Diego Natural History Museum.

No butterfly list is complete—or at least not for long! Be on the lookout for unusual butterflies not pictured here. The joys of butterflying include discovering the unexpected.

FAMILY: Papilionidae

In the caption beneath each butterfly, the flight period refers to the earliest-latest dates reported in "Early/Late California Butterfly Records," 2002, by Stanford *et al.* Page numbers refer to pages where the species is mentioned.

PIPEVINE SWALLOWTAIL
Battus philenor
Size: Large (2³/₄"–4")
Flies: Jan–Nov (see p. 20)

CLOUDED SULPHUR
Colias philodice
Size: Medium (1¹/₂"–2¹/₈")
Flies: Jun–Oct (see p. 32)

SOUTHERN DOGFACE
Zerene (= Colias) cesonia
Size: Med–Large (2¹/₈"–2⁵/₈")
Flies: Feb–Nov (see p. 34)

BOISDUVAL'S YELLOW
Eurema boisduvaliana
Size: Sm–Med (1³/₈"–1⁵/₈")
Flies: Apr–May (see p. 34)

MEXICAN YELLOW
Eurema mexicana
Size: Medium (1¹/₂"–2")
Flies: May–Nov (see p. 34)

MIMOSA YELLOW
Eurema (= Pyrisitia) nise
Size: Small (1¹/₈"–1³/₈")
Flies: Apr–May (See p. 35)

SILVER-BANDED HAIRSTREAK
Chlorostrymon simaethis sarita
Size: Tiny (⁷/₈"–1")
Flies: Apr–Nov

WESTERN PINE ELFIN
Callophrys eryphon
Size: Small (1"–1¹/₈")
Flies: Mar–Sep

GREENISH BLUE
Plebejus saepiolus hilda
Size: Small (1"–1¹/₄")
Flies: May–Aug

GULF FRITILLARY
Agraulis vanillae
Size: Large (2¹/₄"–3¹/₄")
Flies: Jan–Dec (see p. 67)

SILVER-SPOTTED SKIPPER
Epargyreus clarus huachuca
Size: Med–Larg (1³/₄"–2¹/₂")
Flies: Apr–Sep

HAMMOCK SKIPPER
Polygonus leo
Size: Medium (1³/₄"–2¹/₈")
Flies: Aug–Sep

LONG-TAILED SKIPPER
Urbanus proteus
Size: Medium (1³/₄"–1⁷/₈")
Flies: Apr–Oct

ERICHSON'S WHITE SKIPPER
Heliopetes (=Heliopyrgus) domicella
Size: Small (1"–1¹/₄")
Flies: Sep–Oct (see p. 96)

UMBER SKIPPER
Poanes melane
Size: Small (1¹/₄"–1³/₈")
Flies: Jan–Dec

DUN SKIPPER
Euphyes vestris harbisoni
Size: Small (1¹/₈"–1³/₈")
Flies: May–Jul

105

Butterflies & their Caterpillar Food Plants of Anza–Borrego Desert State Park® & Environs

This list was compiled from references and personal communications that are indicated by asterisks on pages 123-124 as well as from the authors' personal observations. We limited plant species to those occurring in our area as listed in *Plants of Anza-Borrego Desert State Park*, 1986, by D. Clemons and *A Flora of San Diego County, California*, 1986, by R. M. Beauchamp.

Swallowtails (PAPILIONIDAE)

'DESERT' BLACK SWALLOWTAIL, *Papilio polyxenes coloro*
    Citrus Family. RUTACEAE: Turpentine Broom, *Thamnosma montana*

ANISE SWALLOWTAIL, *Papilio zelicaon*
    Carrot Family, APIACEAE: Rattlesnake Weed, *Daucus pusillus;* Woolly-Fruit Lomatium, *Lomatium dasycarpum*; Pacific Oenanthe, *Oenanthe sarmentosa*; Southern Tauschia, *Tauschia arguta*

INDRA SWALLOWTAIL, *Papilio indra pergamus*
    Carrot Family, APIACEAE: Shiny Lomatium, *Lomatium lucidum;* Southern Tauschia, *Tauschia arguta*

GIANT SWALLOWTAIL, *Papilio cresphontes*
    Citrus Family, RUTACEAE: Citrus trees, *Citrus* spp.

WESTERN TIGER SWALLOWTAIL, *Papilio rutulus*
    Sycamore Family, PLANTANACEAE: California Sycamore, *Plantanus racemosa*
    Birch Family, BETULACEAE: Mountain Alder, *Alnus rhombifolia*
    Willow Family, SALICACEAE: Slender Willow, *Salix exigua;* Arroyo Willow, *S. lasiolepis*

PALE SWALLOWTAIL, *Papilio eurymedon*
    Buckthorn Family, RHAMNACEAE: Wedgeleaf Ceanothus, *Ceanothus cuneatus;* Hoary Coffeeberry, *Rhamnus tomentella*
    Rose Family, ROSACEAE: Western Chokecherry, *Prunus virginiana;* Hollyleaf Cherry, *P. ilicifolia*

Whites & Sulphurs (PIERIDAE)

BECKER'S WHITE, *Pontia beckerii*
    Caper Family, CAPPARACEAE: Bladderpod, *Isomeris arborea*

SPRING WHITE, *Pontia sisymbrii*
    Mustard Family, BRASSICACEAE: Nevada Rockcress, *Arabis perennans;* Sicklepod Rockcress, *A. sparsiflora*; Payson's Jewelflower, *Caulanthus simulans*; California Mustard, *Guillenia lasiophylla;* Tumble Mustard, *Sisymbrium altissimum*; Jewelflowers, *Streptanthus* spp.

CHECKERED WHITE, *Pontia protodice*
    Mustard Family, BRASSICACEAE: Turnip Mustard, *Brassica tournefortii*; Tansy Mustard, *Descurainia pinnata*; Tumble Mustard, *Sisymbrium altissimum*

CABBAGE WHITE, *Pieris rapae*
    Mustard Family, BRASSICACEAE: Cooper's Caulanthus, *Caulanthus cooperi*; Tumble Mustard, *Sisymbrium altissiumum*; London Rocket, *Sisymbrium irio*

CALIFORNIA MARBLE, *Euchloe hyantis*
    Mustard Family, BRASSICACEAE: Tansy Mustard, *Descurainia pinnata*; California Mustard, *Guillenia lasiophylla*; Jewelflowers, *Streptanthus* spp.

'GRINNELL'S' GRAY MARBLE, *Anthocharis lanceolata australis*
    Mustard Family, BRASSICACEAE: Sicklepod Rockcress, *Arabis sparsiflora*

'DESERT EDGE' GRAY MARBLE, *Anthocharis lanceolata desertolimbus*
 Mustard Family, BRASSICACEAE: Nevada Rockcress, *Arabis perennans*

DESERT ORANGETIP, *Anthocharis cethura*
 Mustard Family, BRASSICACEAE: Cooper's Caulanthus, *Caulanthus cooperi*; Payson's
 Jewelflower, *C. simulans*; Tansy Mustard, *Descurainia pinnata*; Longbeak
 Twistflower, *Streptanthella langisrostris*; Lacepod, *Thysanocarpus curvipes*

SARA ORANGETIP, *Anthocharis sara*
 Mustard Family, BRASSICACEAE: Nevada Rockcress, *Arabis perennans*; Turnip Mustard,
 Brassica tournefortii; Hall's Caulanthus, *Caulanthus hallii*; Payson's Jewelflower, *C.
 simulans;* Tansy Mustard, *Descurainia pinnata*; Lacepod, *Thysanocarpus curvipes*

ORANGE SULPHUR, *Colias eurytheme*
 Pea Family, FABACEAE: Desert Rattlepod, *Astragalus crotalariae*; Deerweed, *Lotus
 scoparius;* Bishop Lotus, *L. strigosus*

HARFORD'S SULPHUR, *Colias harfordii*
 Pea Family, FABACEAE: Parish Locoweed, *Astragalus douglasii* var *parishii*; Palmer
 Locoweed, *A. palmeri*; Deerweed, *Lotus scoparius*

CALIFORNIA DOGFACE, *Zerene eurydice*
 Pea Family, FABACEAE: False Indigo, *Amorpha fruticosa*

DAINTY SULPHUR, *Nathalis iole*
 Sunflower Family, ASTERACEAE: San Felipe Dyssodia, *Adenophyllum porophylloides*;
 Spanish Needles, *Palafoxia arida*; Cinchweed, *Pectis papposa*

SLEEPY ORANGE, *Eurema nicippe*
 Pea Family, FABACEAE: Desert Cassia, *Senna armata*; Coues' Cassia, *S. covesii*

CLOUDLESS SULPHUR, *Phoebis sennae*
 Pea Family, FABACEAE: Desert Cassia, *Senna armata*; Coues' Cassia, *S. covesii*

Coppers, Hairstreaks & *Blues* (LYCAENIDAE)

TAILED COPPER, *Lycaena arota*
 Gooseberry Family, GROSSULARIACEAE: Oakleaf Gooseberry, *Ribes quercetorum*

GORGON COPPER, *Lycaena gorgon*
 Buckwheat Family, POLYGONACEAE: Tall Buckwheat, *Eriogonum elongatum*

GREAT COPPER, *Lycaena xanthoides*
 Buckwheat Family, POLYGONACEAE: Curly Dock, *Rumex crispus*; Willow Dock, *R.
 salicifolius*

PURPLISH COPPER, *Lycaena helloides*
 Buckwheat Family, POLYGONACEAE: Curly Dock, *Rumex crispus*; Willow Dock, *R.
 salicifolius*

GREAT PURPLE HAIRSTREAK, *Atlides halesus*
 Mistletoe Family, VISCACEAE: Desert Mistletoe, *Phoradendron californicum*; Dense
 Mistletoe, *P. densum*; Big Leaf Mistletoe, *P. macrophyllum*

GOLDEN HAIRSTREAK, *Habrodais grunus*
 Oak Family, FAGACEAE: Canyon Live Oak, *Quercus chrysolepis*

GOLD-HUNTER'S HAIRSTREAK, *Satyrium auretorum*
 Oak Family, FAGACEAE: Canyon Live Oak, *Quercus chrysolepis*; Desert Scrub Oak, *Q.
 cornelius–mulleri*; Scrub Live Oak, *Quercus wislizeni* var *frutescens*

HEDGEROW HAIRSTREAK, *Satyrium saepium*
  Buckthorn Family, RHAMNACEAE: Wedgeleaf Ceanothus, *Ceanothus cuneatus;* Cupleaf Ceanothus, *C. greggii;* Chaparral Whitethorn, *C. leucodermis;* Hairy Ceanothus, *C. oliganthus*

SYLVAN HAIRSTREAK, *Satyrium sylvinus*
  Willow Family, SALICACEAE: Slender Willow, *Salix exigua;* Arroyo Willow, *S. lasiolepis*

CALIFORNIA HAIRSTREAK, *Satyrium californica*
  Buckthorn Family, RHAMNACEAE: Wedgeleaf Ceanothus, *Ceanothus cuneatus*
  Oak Family, FAGACEAE: Scrub Live Oak, *Quercus wislizeni* var *frutescens*
  Rose Family, ROSACEAE: Mountain-Mahogany, *Cercocarpus betuloides;* Western Chokecherry, *Prunus virginiana*
  Willow Family, SALICACEAE: Willows, *Salix* spp

MOUNTAIN MAHOGANY HAIRSTREAK, *Satyrium tetra*
  Rose Family, ROSACEAE: Mountain-Mahogany, *Cercocarpus betuloides*

'LOKI' JUNIPER HAIRSTREAK, *Callophrys gryneus loki*
  Cypress Family, CUPRESSACEAE: California Juniper, *Juniperus californica*

NELSON'S HAIRSTREAK, *Callophrys nelsoni*
  Cypress Family, CUPRESSACEAE: Incensecedar, *Calocedrus decurrens*

THICKET HAIRSTREAK, *Callophrys spinetorum*
  Mistletoe Family, VISCACAE: Western Dwarf Mistletoe, *Arceuthobium campylopodum;* Pinyon Dwarf Mistletoe, *A. divaricatum*

BROWN ELFIN, *Callophrys augustinus*
  Buckthorn Family, RHAMNACEAE: Cupleaf Ceanothus, *Ceanothus greggii;* Chaparral Whitethorn, *C. leucodermis;* Hollyleaf Redberry, *Rhamnus ilicifolia;* Hoary Coffeeberry, *R. tomentella*
  Dodder Family, CUSCUTACEAE: Dodder, *Cuscuta* spp.
  Rose Family, ROSACEAE: Chamise, *Adenostoma fasciculatum;* Hollyleaf Cherry, *Prunus ilicifolia*

BRAMBLE HAIRSTREAK, *Callophrys perplexa*
  Buckwheat Family, POLYGONACEAE: Tall Buckwheat, *Eriogonum elongatum;* Buckwheat, *E. fasciculatum*
  Pea Family, FABACEAE: Deerweed, *Lotus scoparius;* Bishop Lotus, *L. strigosus*

MALLOW SCRUB-HAIRSTREAK, *Strymon istapa*
  Mallow Family, MALVACEAE: Rock Hibiscus, *Hibiscus denudatus*

GRAY HAIRSTREAK, *Strymon melinus*
  Buckwheat Family, POLYGONACEAE: Davidson Buckwheat, *Eriogonum davidsonii;* Tall Buckwheat, *E. elongatum;* Desert Trumpet, *E. inflatum;* Knotty Buckwheat, *E. wrightii* var *nodosum* and/or Foothill Buckwheat, *E. wrightii* var *membranaceum*
  Mallow Family, MALVACEAE: Rock Hibiscus, *Hibiscus denudatus;* Cheeseweed, *Malva parviflora;* Apricot Mallow, *Sphaeralcea ambigua*
  Mint Family, LAMIACEAE: Desert Lavender, *Hyptis emoryi*
  Pea Family, FABACEAE: Deerweed, *Lotus scoparius;* Desert Cassia, *Senna armata*
  Stonecrop Family, CRASSULACEAE: Desert Dudleya, *Dudleya saxosa*
  Sunflower Family, ASTERACEAE: Western Sunflower, *Helianthus annuus*
  Willow Family, SALICACEAE: Willows, *Salix* spp

LEDA MINISTREAK, *Ministrymon leda*
  Pea Family, FABACEAE: Honey Mesquite, *Prosopis glandulosa*

MARINE BLUE, *Leptotes marina*
 Pea Family, FABACEAE: Catclaw, *Acacia greggii;* False Indigo, *Amorpha fruticosa;*
  Deerweed, *Lotus scoparius;* Honey Mesquite, *Prosopis glandulosa;* Screwbean Mesquite,
  P. pubescens
 Rose Family, ROSACEAE: Chamise, *Adenostoma fasciculatum*

REAKIRT'S BLUE, *Hemiargus isola*
 Pea Family, FABACEAE: Catclaw, *Acacia greggii;* Honey Mesquite, *Prosopis glandulosa;*
  Screwbean Mesquite, *P. pubescens*

CERAUNUS BLUE, *Hemiargus ceraunus*
 Pea Family, FABACEAE: Catclaw, *Acacia greggii;* Desert Rattlepod, *Astragalus crotalariae;*
  Parish Locoweed, *A. douglasii* var *parishii;* Palmer Locoweed, *A. palmeri;* Honey
  Mesquite, *Prosopis glandulosa;* Screwbean Mesquite, *P. pubescens.*
 Buckwheat Family, POLYGONACEAE: Davidson Buckwheat, *Eriogonum davidsonii;* Tall
  Buckwheat, *E. elongatum;* Desert Trumpet, *E. inflatum;* Kidneyleaf Buckwheat, *E.
  reniforme;* Knotty Buckwheat, *E. wrightii* var *nodosum* and/or Foothill Buckwheat, *E.
  wrightii* var *membranaceum*

WESTERN PIGMY BLUE, *Brephidium exile*
 Goosefoot Family, CHENOPODIACEAE: Fourwing Saltbush, *Atriplex canescens;* Desert
  Holly, *A. hymenelytra;* California Goosefoot, *Chenopodium californicum;* White
  Pigweed, *C. murale;* Russian Thistle, *Salsola tragus.*

WESTERN TAILED BLUE, *Everes amyntula*
 Pea Family, FABACEAE: Parish Locoweed, *Astragalus douglasii;* Palmer Locoweed, *A. palmeri*

SPRING AZURE, *Celastrina ladon echo*
 Buckthorn Family, RHAMNACEAE: Chaparral Whitethorn, *Ceanothus leucodermis;* Hoary
  Coffeeberry, *Rhamnus tomentella*
 Rose Family, ROSACEAE: Chamise, *Adenostoma fasciculatum;* Hollyleaf Cherry, *Prunus ilicifolia*
 Sunflower Family, ASTERACEAE: Mulefat, *Baccharis salicifolia*

BERNARDINO DOTTED-BLUE, *Euphilotes bernardino*
 Buckwheat Family, POLYGONACEAE: Buckwheat, *Eriogonum fasciculatum*

'DAMMER'S' DOTTED-BLUE, *Euphilotes enoptes dammersi*
 Buckwheat Family, POLYGONACEAE: Tall Buckwheat, *Eriogonum elongatum;* Knotty
  Buckwheat, *E. wrightii* var *nodosum;* Foothill Buckwheat, *E. wrightii* var
  membranaceum

'PRATT'S' DOTTED-BLUE, *Euphilotes enoptes cryptorufes*
 Buckwheat Family, POLYGONACEAE: Davidson Buckwheat, *Eriogonum davidsonii*

MOJAVE DOTTED-BLUE, *Euphilotes mojave*
 Buckwheat Family, POLYGONACEAE: Kidneyleaf Buckwheat, *Eriogonum reniforme*

SMALL BLUE, *Philotiella speciosa*
 Buckwheat Family, POLYGONACEAE: Kidneyleaf Buckwheat, *Eriogonum reniforme*

SONORAN BLUE, *Philotes sonorensis*
 Stonecrop Family, CRASSULACEAE: Desert Dudleya, *Dudleya saxona*

SILVERY BLUE, *Glaucopsyche lygdamus australis*
 Pea Family, FABACEAE: Parish Locoweed, *Astragalus douglasii* var *parishii;* Desert Lotus,
  Lotus rigidus; Deerweed, *L. scoparius;* Grape Soda Lupine, *Lupinus excubitus;*
  Adonis Lupine, *L. formosus*

ARROWHEAD BLUE, *Glaucopsyche piasus umbrosa*

Pea Family, FABACEAE: Adonis Lupine, *Lupinus formosus*

BOISDUVAL'S BLUE, *Plebejus icarioides evius*
Pea Family, FABACEAE: Grape Soda Lupine, *Lupinus excubitus;* Adonis Lupine, *L. formosus*

ACMON BLUE, *Plebejus acmon*
Buckwheat Family, POLYGONACEAE: Davidson Buckwheat, *Eriogonum davidsonii;* Tall Buckwheat, *E. elongatum*; Buckwheat, *E. fasciculatum;* Kidneyleaf Buckwheat, *E. reniforme*; Knotty Buckwheat, *E. wrightii* var *nodosum* and/or Foothill Buckwheat, *E. wrightii* var *membranaceum*
Pea Family, FABACEAE: Nevada Lotus, *Lotus nevadensis*; Spanish Clover, *L. purshianus*; Deerweed, *L. scoparius;* Bishop Lotus, *L. strigosus;* Miniature Lupine, *Lupinus bicolor*

LUPINE BLUE, *Plebejus lupini monticola*
Buckwheat Family, POLYGONACEAE: Buckwheat, *Eriogonum fasciculatum*; Knotty Buckwheat, *E. wrightii* var *nodosum* and/or Foothill Buckwheat, *E. wrightii* var *membranaceum*

MELISSA BLUE, *Lycaeides melissa*
Pea Family, FABACEAE: Parish Locoweed, *Astragalus douglasii* var *parishii*; Nevada Lotus, *Lotus nevadensis*; Spanish Clover, *L. purshianus;* Grape Soda Lupine, *Lupinus excubitus*

Metalmarks (RIODINIDAE)
WRIGHT'S METALMARK, *Calephelis wrighti*
Sunflower Family, ASTERACEAE: Sweetbush, *Bebbia juncea*

DESERT METALMARK, *Apodemia mejicanus deserti*
Buckwheat Family, POLYGONACEAE: Desert Trumpet, *Eriogonum inflatum*; Buckwheat, *E. fasciculatum* (probably)

BEHR'S METALMARK, *Apodemia virgulti*
Buckwheat Family, POLYGONACEAE: Buckwheat, *Eriogonum fasciculatum*

'PENINSULAR' MORMON METALMARK, *Apodemia mormo peninsularis*
Buckwheat Family, POLYGONACEAE: Foothill Buckwheat, *Eriogonum wrightii* var *membranaceum*

PALMER'S METALMARK, *Apodemia palmeri*
Pea Family, FABACEAE: Honey Mesquite, *Prosopis glandulosa*; Screwbean Mesquite, *P. pubescens*

Brushfoots (NYMPHALIDAE)
AMERICAN SNOUT, *Libytheana carinenta*
Elm Family, ULMACEAE: Netleaf Hackberry, *Celtis reticulata*

VARIEGATED FRITILLARY, *Euptoieta claudia*
Violet Family, VIOLACEAE: Violets, *Viola* spp. Possibly other food plants and families.

CALLIPPE FRITILLARY, *Speyeria callippe comstocki*
Violet Family, VIOLACEAE: Mountain Violet, *Viola purpurea*

CORONIS FRITILLARY, *Speyeria coronis semiramis*
Violet Family, VIOLACEAE: Mountain Violet, *Viola purpurea*

TINY CHECKERSPOT, *Dymasia dymas imperialis*
Acanthus Family, ACANTHACEAE: Chuparosa, *Justicia californica*

CALIFORNIA PATCH, *Chlosyne californica*
Sunflower Family, ASTERACEAE: Parish Viguieria, *Viguiera parishii*; occasionally Western Sunflower, *Helianthus annuus*

BORDERED PATCH, *Chlosyne lacinia crocale*
Sunflower Family, ASTERACEAE: Western Sunflower, *Helianthus annuus*; Parish Viguiera, *Viguieria parishii*

GABB'S CHECKERSPOT, *Chlosyne gabbii*
Sunflower Family, ASTERACEAE: Sawtooth Goldenbush, *Hazardia squarrosa* ssp. *grindelioides*; Cudweed Aster, *Lessingia filaginifolia*

'NEUMOEGEN'S' SAGEBRUSH CHECKERSPOT, *Chlosyne acastus neumoegeni*
Sunflower Family, ASTERACEAE: Desert Goldenhead, *Acamptopappus sphaerocephalus*; Orcutt's Aster, *Xylorhiza orcuttii*

LEANIRA CHECKERSPOT, *Chlosyne leanira wrighti*
Snapdragon Family, SCROPHULARIACEAE: Woolly Indian Paintbrush, *Castilleja foliolosa*

'HENNE'S' VARIABLE CHECKERSPOT, *Euphydryas chalcedona hennei*
Snapdragon Family, SCROPHULARIACEAE: Woolly Indian Paintbrush, *Castilleja foliolosa*; Desert Bushpenstemon, *Keckiella antirrhinoides*

QUINO CHECKERSPOT, *Euphydryas editha quino*
Plantain Family, PLANTAGINACEAE: Southwestern Plantain, *Plantago patagonica*
Snapdragon Family, SCROPHULARIACEAE: White Snapdragon, *Antirrhinum coulterianum*, Purple Owl's Clover, *Castilleja exserta*

MYLITTA CRESECENT, *Phyciodes mylitta*
Sunflower Family, ASTERACEAE: Thistles, *Cirsium* spp
Snapdragon Family, SCROPHULARIACEAE: Seep Monkeyflower, *Mimulus guttatus*

SATYR COMMA, *Polygonia satyrus*
Nettle Family, URTICACEAE: Hoary Nettle, *Urtica dioica* ssp *holosericea*

RED ADMIRAL, *Vanessa atalanta*
Nettle Family, URTICACEAE: Hoary Nettle, *Urtica dioica* ssp *holosericea*

PAINTED LADY, *Vanessa cardui*
Borage Family, BORAGACEAE: Fiddleneck, *Amsinckia tessellata,* Cryptantha, *Cryptantha* spp
Mallow Family, MALVACEAE: Cheeseweed, *Malva parviflora*
Nettle Family, URTICACEAE: Hoary Nettle, *Urtica dioica* ssp *holosericea*
Pea Family, FABACEAE: Arizona Lupine, *Lupinus arizonicus*, Indigobush, *Psorothamnus schottii*
Plantain Family, PLANTAGINACEAE: Woolly Plantain, *Plantago ovata*
Sunflower Family, ASTERACEAE: Bird's Nest Thistle, *Cirsium scariosum*; Desert Dicoria, *Dicoria canescens*

WEST COAST LADY, *Vanessa annabella*
Mallow Family, MALVACEAE: Apricot Mallow, *Sphaeralcea ambigua*
Nettle Family, URTICACEAE: Hoary Nettle, *Urtica dioica* ssp *holosericea*

AMERICAN LADY, *Vanessa virginiensis*
Sunflower Family, ASTERACEAE: Everlastings, *Gnaphalium* spp

CALIFORNIA TORTOISESHELL, *Nymphalis californica*
Buckthorn Family, RHAMNACEAE: Wedgeleaf Ceanothus, *Ceanothus cuneatus*

MOURNING CLOAK, *Nymphalis antiopa*
Willow Family, SALICACEAE: Fremont Cottonwood, *Populus fremontii*; Slender Willow, *Salix exigua*

COMMON BUCKEYE, *Junonia coenia*
Plantain Family, PLANTAGINACEAE: Southwestern Plantain, *Plantago patigonica*
Snapdragon Family, SCROPHULARIACEAE: White Snapdragon, *Antirrhinum coulterianum*;

Purple Owl's Clover, *Castilleja exserta*

COMMON RINGLET, *Coenonympha tullia california*
   Grass Family, POACEAE: Needlegrasses, *Stipa* spp; Kentucky Blue Grass, *Poa pratensis*

GREAT BASIN WOOD-NYMPH, *Cercyonis sthenele silvestris*
   Grass Family, POACEAE: Squirreltail, *Elymus elymoides* (probably)

LORQUIN'S ADMIRAL, *Limenitis lorquini*
   Rose Family, ROSACEAE: Western Chokecherry, *Prunus virginiana*
   Willow Family, SALICACEAE: Arroyo Willow, *S. lasiolepis*; other Willows, *Salix* spp, probably
      including Slender Willow, *S. exigua* and Largeleaf Willow, *S. laevigata*

CALIFORNIA SISTER, *Adelpha bredowii californica*
   Oak Family, FAGACEAE: California Live Oak, *Quercus agrifolia*; Canyon Live Oak, *Q. chrysolepis*; California Black Oak, *Q. kelloggii*; Scrub Live Oak, *Q. wislizeni* var *frutescens*

MONARCH, *Danaus plexippus*
   Milkweed Family, ASCLEPIADACEAE: California Milkweed, *Asclepias californica*; Desert
      Milkweed, *A. erosa*

QUEEN, *Danaus gilippus*
   Milkweed Family, ASCLEPIADACEAE: White–stemmed Milkweed, *Asclepias albicans*; Desert
      Milkweed, *A. erosa*; Rush Milkweed, *A. subulata*; Climbing Milkvine, *Sarcostemma cynanchoides* ssp *hartwegii*; Smooth Milkvine, *Sarcostemma hirtellum*

Skippers (HESPERIIDAE)

ARIZONA POWDERED-SKIPPER, *Systasea zampa*
   Mallow Family, MALVACEAE: Palmer Abutilon, *Abutilon palmeri*; Rock Hibiscus,
      Hibiscus denudatus; Yellow Feltplant, *Horsfordia newberryi*

NORTHERN CLOUDYWING, *Thorybes pylades*
   Pea Family, FABACEAE: False Indigo, *Amorpha fruticosa*; other peas.

SLEEPY DUSKYWING, *Erynnis brizo lacustra*
   Oak Family, FAGACEAE: Desert Scrub Oak, *Quercus cornelius-mulleri*

AFRANIUS DUSKYWING, *Erynnis afranius*
   Pea Family, FABACEAE: Nevada Lotus, *Lotus nevadensis*; Spanish Clover, *L. purshianus*

PACUVIUS DUSKYWING, *Erynnis pacuvius*
   Buckthorn Family, RHAMNACEAE: Cupleaf Ceanothus, *C. greggii* (probably); Hairy
      Ceanothus, *C. oliganthus*

FUNEREAL DUSKYWING, *Erynnis funeralis*
   Pea Family, FABACEAE: Deerweed, *Lotus scoparius*; Desert Ironwood, *Olneya tesota;*
      many other peas

MOURNFUL DUSKYWING, *Erynnis tristis*
   Oak Family, FAGACEAE: California Live Oak, *Quercus agrifolia;* Scrub Live Oak,
      Q. wislizeni var *frutescens;* Desert Scrub Oak, *Q. cornelius-mulleri* (probably)

PROPERTIUS DUSKYWING, *Erynnis propertius*
   Oak Family, FAGACEAE: California Live Oak, *Quercus agrifolia*; probably other oaks

MOJAVE SOOTYWING, *Hesperopsis libya*
   Goosefoot Family, CHENOPODIACEAE: Fourwing Saltbush, *Atriplex canescens*

COMMON SOOTYWING, *Pholisora catullus*
   Amaranth Family, AMARANTHACEAE: Fringe Amaranth, *Amaranthus fimbriatus*
   Goosefoot Family, CHENOPODIACEAE: California Goosefoot, *Chenopodium*

californicum; White Pigweed, *C. murale*

WHITE CHECKERED-SKIPPER, *Pyrgus albescens*
    Mallow Family, MALVACEAE: Desert Fivespot, *Eremalche rotundifolia*; Cheeseweed, *Malva parviflora*; Apricot Mallow, *Sphaeralcea ambigua*

SMALL CHECKERED-SKIPPER, *Pyrgus scriptura*
    Mallow Family, MALVACEAE: Apricot Mallow, *Sphaeralcea ambigua*

'LAGUNA' TWO-BANDED CHECKERED-SKIPPER, *Pyrgus ruralis lagunae*
    Rose Family, ROSACEAE: Cleveland's Horkelia, *Horkelia clevelandii*

NORTHERN WHITE-SKIPPER, *Heliopetes ericetorum*
    Mallow Family, MALVACEAE: Desert Fivespot, *Eremalche rotundifolia;* Rock Hibiscus, *Hibiscus denudatus*; Shrub Globemallow, *Malacothamnus densiflorus* (probably); Apricot Mallow, *Sphaeralcea ambigua*

EUFALA SKIPPER, *Lerodea eufala*
    Grass Family, POACEAE: Bermuda Grass, *Cynodon dactylon*

SACHEM, *Atalopedes campestris*
    Grass Family, POACEAE: Bermuda Grass, *Cynodon dactylon;* Kentucky Bluegrass, *Poa pratensis*

JUBA SKIPPER, *Hesperia juba*
    Grass Family, POACEAE: Red Brome, *Bromus madritensis* ssp *rubens*; Kentucky Bluegrass, *Poa pratensis*

WESTERN BRANDED SKIPPER, *Hesperia colorado leussleri*
    Grass Family, POACEAE: Tufted Fescue, *Vulpia octoflora* var *hirtella* (probably)

COLUMBIA SKIPPER, *Hesperia columbia*
    Grass Family, POACEAE: Junegrass, *Koeleria macrantha*

LINDSEY SKIPPER, *Hesperia lindseyi*
    Grass Family, POACEAE: California Oatgrass, *Danthonia californica*

ORANGE SKIPPERLING, *Copaeodes aurantiacus*
    Grass Family, POACEAE: Bermuda Grass, *Cynodon dactylon*

ALKALI SKIPPER, *Pseudocopaeodes eunus*
    Grass Family, POACEAE: Desert Saltgrass, *Distichlis spicata* var *stricta*

SANDHILL SKIPPER, *Polites sabuleti*
    Grass Family, POACEAE: Desert Saltgrass, *Distichlis spicata* var *stricta*

FIERY SKIPPER, *Hylephila phyleus*
    Grass Family, POACEAE: Bermuda Grass, *Cynodon dactylon;* Kentucky Bluegrass, *Poa pratensis*

RURAL SKIPPER, *Ochlodes agricola*
    Grass Family, POACEAE: Grasses

WOODLAND SKIPPER, *Ochlodes sylvanoides*
    Grass Family, POACEAE: Bermuda Grass, *Cynodon dactylon*

CALIFORNIA GIANT-SKIPPER, *Agathymus stephensi*
    Lily Family, LILIACEAE: Desert Agave, *Agave deserti*

YUCCA GIANT-SKIPPER, *Megathymus yuccae harbisoni*
    Lily Family, LILIACEAE: Mojave Yucca, *Yucca schidigera*

Caterpillar Food Plants & Butterfly Species of Anza–Borrego Desert State Park® & Environs

This list of 140 caterpillar food plants, 121 of which are pictured in this book, was compiled from references and personal communications that are indicated by asterisks on pages 123-124 as well as from the authors' personal observations. We limited plant species to those occurring in our area as listed in *Plants of Anza-Borrego Desert State Park*, 1986, by D. Clemons and *A Flora of San Diego County, California*, 1986, by R. M. Beauchamp.

Food Plants

Butterfly Species

ACANTHUS FAMILY, ACANTHACEAE
Chuparosa, *Justicia californica* — Tiny Checkerspot, *Dymasia dymas imperialis*

AMARANTH FAMILY, AMARANTHACEAE
Fringe Amaranth, *Amaranthus fimbriatus* — Common Sootywing, *Pholisora catullus*

BIRCH FAMILY, BETULACEAE
Mountain Alder, *Alnus rhombifolia* — Western Tiger Swallowtail, *Papilio rutulus*

BORAGE FAMILY, BORAGINACEAE
Fiddleneck, *Amsinckia tessellata* — Painted Lady, *Vanessa cardui*

Cryptantha, *Cryptantha* spp. — Painted Lady, *Vanessa cardui*

BUCKTHORN FAMILY, RHAMNACEAE
Wedgeleaf Ceanothus, *Ceanothus cuneatus* — Pale Swallowtail, *Papilio eurymedon*
Hedgerow Hairstreak, *Satyrium saepium*
California Hairstreak, *Satyrium californica*
California Tortoiseshell, *Nymphalis californica*

Cupleaf Ceanothus, *Ceanothus greggii* — Hedgerow Hairstreak, *Satyrium saepium*
Brown Elfin, *Callophrys augustinus*
Pacuvius Duskywing, *Erynnis pacuvius* (prob)

Chaparral Whitethorn, *Cean. leucodermis* — Hedgerow Hairstreak, *Satyrium saepium*
Brown Elfin, *Callophrys augustinus*
Spring Azure, *Celastrina ladon echo*

Hairy Ceanothus, *Ceanothus oliganthus* — Hedgerow Hairstreak, *Satyrium saepium*
Pacuvius Duskywing, *Erynnis pacuvius*

Hollyleaf Redberry, *Rhamnus ilicifolia* — Brown Elfin, *Callophrys augustinus*

Hoary Coffeeberry, *Rhamnus tomentella* — Pale Swallowtail, *Papilio eurymedon*
Brown Elfin, *Callophrys augustinus*
Spring Azure, *Celastrina ladon echo*

BUCKWHEAT FAMILY, POLYGONACEAE
Davidson Buckwheat, *Eriogonum davidsonii* — Gray Hairstreak, *Strymon melinus*
Ceraunus Blue, *Hemiargus ceraunus*
'Pratt's' Dotted-Blue, *Euphilotes enoptes cryptorufes*
Acmon Blue, *Plebejus acmon*

Tall Buckwheat, *Eriogonum elongatum*	Gorgon Copper, *Lycaena gorgon*
	Bramble Hairstreak, *Callophrys perplexa*
	Gray Hairstreak, *Strymon melinus*
	Ceraunus Blue, *Hemiargus ceraunus*
	'Dammer's' Dotted-Blue, *Euphilotes enoptes dammersi*
	Acmon Blue, *Plebejus acmon*
Buckwheat, *Eriogonum fasciculatum*	Bramble Hairstreak, *Callophrys perplexa*
	Bernardino Dotted-Blue, *Euphilotes bernardino*
	Acmon Blue, *Plebejus acmon*
	Lupine Blue, *Plebejus lupini monticola*
	Desert Metalmark, *Apodemia mejicanus deserti* (probably)
	Behr's Metalmark, *Apodemia virgulti*
Desert Trumpet, *Eriogonum inflatum*	Gray Hairstreak, *Strymon melinus*
	Ceraunus Blue, *Hemiargus ceraunus*
	Desert Metalmark, *Apodemia mejicanus deserti*
Kidneyleaf Buckwheat, *Eriogonum reniforme*	Ceraunus Blue, *Hemiargus ceraunus*
	Mojave Dotted-Blue, *Euphilotes mojave*
	Small Blue, *Philotiella speciosa*
	Acmon Blue, *Plebejus acmon*
Knotty Buckwheat, *Eriogonum wrightii* var *nodosum* and/or Foothill Buckwheat, *Eriogonum wrightii* var *membranaceum*	Gray Hairstreak, *Strymon melinus*
	Ceraunus Blue, *Hemiargus ceraunus*
	'Dammer's' Dotted-Blue, *Euphilotes enoptes dammersi*
	Acmon Blue, *Plebejus acmon*
	Lupine Blue, *Plebejus lupini monticola*
Foothill Buckwheat, *Eriogonum wrightii* var *membranaceum*	'Peninsular' Mormon Metalmark, *Apodemia mormo peninsularis*
Curly Dock, *Rumex crispus*	Great Copper, *Lycaena xanthoides*
	Purplish Copper, *Lycaena helloides*
Willow Dock, *Rumex salicifolius*	Great Copper, *Lycaena xanthoides*
	Purplish Copper, *Lycaena helloides*

CAPER FAMILY, CAPPARACEAE
  Bladderpod, *Isomeris arborea* — Becker's White, *Pontia beckerii*

CARROT FAMILY, APIACEAE
  Rattlesnake Weed, *Daucus pusillus* — Anise Swallowtail, *Papilio zelicaon*

  Woolly-Fruit Lomatium, *Lomatium dasycarpum* — Anise Swallowtail, *Papilio zelicaon*

  Shiny Lomatium, *Lomatium lucidum* — Indra Swallowtail, *Papilio indra pergamus*

  Pacific Oenanthe, *Oenanthe sarmentosa* — Anise Swallowtail, *Papilio zelicaon*

  Southern Tauschia, *Tauschia arguta* — Anise Swallowtail, *Papilio zelicaon*
  Indra Swallowtail, *Papilio indra pergamus*

CITRUS FAMILY, RUTACEAE
Orange, Lemon, etc., *Citrus* spp — Giant Swallowtail, *Papilio cresphontes*

Turpentine Broom, *Thamnosma montana* — 'Desert' Black Swallowtail, *Papilio polyxenes coloro*

CYPRESS FAMILY, CUPRESSACEAE
Incensecedar, *Calocedrus decurrens* — Nelson's Hairstreak, *Callophrys nelsoni*

California Juniper, *Juniperus californica* — 'Loki' Juniper Hairstreak, *Callophrys gryneus loki*

DODDER FAMILY, CUSCATACEAE
Dodder, *Cuscuta* spp — Brown Elfin, *Callophrys augustinus*

ELM FAMILY, ULMACEAE
Netleaf Hackberry, *Celtis reticulata* — American Snout, *Libytheana carinenta*

GOOSEBERRY FAMILY, GROSSULARIACEAE
Oakleaf Gooseberry, *Ribes quercetorum* — Tailed Copper, *Lycaena arota*

GOOSEFOOT FAMILY, CHENOPODIACEAE
Fourwing Saltbush, *Atriplex canescens* — Western Pygmy Blue, *Brephidium exile*
Mojave Sootywing, *Hesperopsis libya*

Desert Holly, *Atriplex hymenelytra* — Western Pygmy Blue, *Brephidium exile*

California Goosefoot, *Chenopodium californicum* — Western Pygmy Blue, *Brephidium exile*
Common Sootywing, *Pholisora catullus*

White Pigweed, *Chenopodium murale* — Western Pygmy Blue, *Brephidium exile*
Common Sootywing, *Pholisora catullus*

Russian Thistle, *Salsola tragus* — Western Pygmy Blue, *Brephidium exile*

GRASS FAMILY, POACEAE
Red Brome, *Bromus madritensis* ssp *rubens* — Juba Skipper, *Hesperia juba*

Bermuda Grass, *Cynodon dactylon* — Eufala Skipper, *Lerodea eufala*
Sachem, *Atalopedes campestris*
Orange Skipperling, *Copaeodes aurantiacus*
Fiery Skipper, *Hylephila phyleus*
Woodland Skipper, *Ochlodes sylvanoides*

California Oatgrass, *Danthonia californica* — Lindsey's Skipper, *Hesperia lindseyi*

Desert Salt Grass, *Distichlis spicata* var *stricta* — Alkali Skipper, *Pseudocopaeodes eunus*
Sandhill skipper, *Polites sabuleti*

Squirreltail, *Elymus elymoides* — Great Basin Wood-Nymph, *Cercyonis sthenele silvestris* (probably)

Junegrass, *Koeleria macrantha* — Columbia Skipper, *Hesperia columbia*

Kentucky Blue Grass, *Poa pratensis* — Common Ringlet, *Coenonympha tullia california*
Sachem, *Atalopedes campestris*
Juba Skipper, *Hesperia juba*

116

Kentucky Blue Grass, *Poa pratensis* (cont.)   Fiery Skipper, *Hylephila phyleus*

Needlegrasses, *Stipa* spp   Common Ringlet, *Coenonympha tullia california*

Tufted Fescue, *Vulpia octoflora* var *hirtella*   Western Branded Skipper, *Hesperia colorado leussleri* (probably)

LILY FAMILY, LILIACEAE
Desert Agave, *Agave deserti*   California Giant-Skipper, *Agathymus stephensi*

Mojave Yucca, *Yucca schidigera*   Yucca Giant-Skipper, *Megathymus yuccae harbisoni*

MALLOW FAMILY, MALVACEAE
Palmer Abutilon, *Abutilon palmeri*   Arizona Powdered-Skipper, *Systasea zampa*

Desert Fivespot, *Eremalche rotundifolia*   White Checkered-Skipper, *Pyrgus albescens*
Northern White-Skipper, *Heliopetes ericetorum*

Rock Hibiscus, *Hibiscus denudatus*   Mallow Scrub-Hairstreak, *Strymon istapa*
Gray Hairstreak, *Strymon melinus*
Arizona Powdered-Skipper, *Systasea zampa*
Northern White-Skipper, *Heliopetes ericetorum*

Yellow Feltplant, *Horsfordia newberryi*   Arizona Powdered-Skipper, *Systasea zampa*

Shrub Globemallow, *Malacothamnus densiflorus*   Northern White-Skipper, *Heliopetes ericetorum* (probably)

Cheeseweed, *Malva parviflora*   Gray Hairstreak, *Strymon melinus*
Painted Lady, *Vanessa cardui*
West Coast Lady, *Vanessa annabella*
White Checkered-Skipper, *Pyrgus albescens*

Apricot Mallow, *Sphaeralcea ambigua*   Gray Hairstreak, *Strymon melinus*
West Coast Lady, *Vanessa annabella*
White Checkered-Skipper, *Pyrgus albescens*
Small Checkered-Skipper, *Pyrgus scriptura*
Northern White-Skipper, *Heliopetes ericetorum*

MILKWEED FAMILY, ASCLEPIADACEAE
White-stemmed Milkweed, *Asclepias albicans*   Queen, *Danaus gilippus*

California Milkweed, *Asclepias californica*   Monarch, *Danaus plexippus*

Desert Milkweed, *Asclepias erosa*   Monarch, *Danaus plexippus*
Queen, *Danaus gilippus*

Rush Milkweed, *Asclepias subulata*   Queen, *Danaus gilippus*

Climbing Milkvine, *Sarcostemma cyanchoides* ssp *hartwegii*   Queen, *Danaus gilippus*

Smooth Milkvine, *Sarcostemma hirtellum*   Queen, *Danaus gilippus*

117

Caterpillar Food Plants & Butterfly Species

MINT FAMILY, LAMIACEAE
Desert Lavender, *Hyptis emoryi* — Gray Hairstreak, *Strymon melinus*

MISTLETOE FAMILY, VISCACEAE
Western Dwarf Mistletoe, *Arceuthobium campylopodum* — Thicket Hairstreak, *Callophrys spinetorum*

Pinyon Dwarf Mistletoe, *A. divaricatum* — Thicket Hairstreat, *Callophrys spinetorum*

Dense Mistletoe, *Phoradendron densum* — Great Purple Hairstreak, *Atlides halesus*

Desert Mistletoe, *Phoradendron californicum* — Great Purple Hairstreak, *Atlides halesus*

Big Leaf Mistletoe, *P. macrophyllum* — Great Purple Hairstreak, *Atlides halesus*

MUSTARD FAMILY, BRASSICACEAE
Nevada Rockcress, *Arabis perennans* — Spring White, *Pontia sisymbrii*; 'Desert Edge' Gray Marble, *Anthocharis lanceolata desertolimbus*; Sara Orangetip, *Anthocharis sara*

Sicklepod Rockcress, *Arabis sparsiflora* — Spring White, *Pontia sisymbrii*; 'Grinnell's' Gray Marble, *Anthocharis lanceolata australis*

Turnip mustard, *Brassica tournifortii* — Checkered White, *Pontia protodice*; Sara Orangetip, *Anthocharis sara*

Cooper's Caulanthus, *Caulanthus cooperi* — Cabbage White, *Pieris rapae*; Desert Orangetip, *Anthocharis cethura*

Hall's Caulanthus, *Caulanthus hallii* — Sara Orangetip, *Anthocharis sara*

Payson's Jewelflower, *Caulanthus simulans* — Spring White, *Pontia sisymbrii*; Desert Orangetip, *Anthocharis cethura*; Sara Orangetip, *Anthocharis sara*

Tansy Mustard, *Descurainia pinnata* — Checkered White, *Pontia protodice*; California Marble, *Euchloe hyantis*; Desert Orangetip, *Anthocharis cethura*; Sara Orangetip, *Anthocharis sara*

California Mustard, *Guillenia lasiophylla* — Spring White, *Pontia sisymbrii*; California Marble, *Euchloe hyantis*

Tumble Mustard, *Sisymbrium altissimum* — Spring White, *Pontia sisymbrii*; Checkered White, *Pontia protodice*; Cabbage White, *Pieris rapae*

London Rocket, *Sisymbrium irio* — Cabbage White, *Pieris rapae*

Longbeak Twistflower, *Streptanthella longirostris* — Desert Orangetip, *Anthocharis cethura*

Jewelflowers, *Streptanthus* spp — Spring White, *Pontia sisymbrii*; California Marble, *Euchloe hyantis*

Lacepod, *Thysanocarpus curvipes*

Desert Orangetip, *Anthocharis cethura*
Sara Orangetip, *Anthocharis sara*

NETTLE FAMILY, URTICACEAE
Hoary Nettle, *Urtica dioicia* ssp *holosericea*

Satyr Comma, *Polygonia satyrus*
Red Admiral, *Vanessa atalanta*
Painted Lady, *Vanessa cardui*
West Coast Lady, *Vanessa annabella*

OAK FAMILY, FAGACEAE
California Live Oak, *Quercus agrifolia*

California Sister, *Adelpha bredowii californica*
Mournful Duskywing, *Erynnis tristis*
Propertius Duskywing, *Erynnis propertius*

Canyon Live Oak, *Quercus chrysolepis*

Golden Hairstreak, *Habrodais grunus*
Gold-hunter's Hairstreak, *Satyrium auretorum*
California Sister, *Adelpha bredowii californica*

Desert Scrub Oak, *Quercus cornelius-mulleri*

Gold-hunter's Hairstreak, *Satyrium auretorum*
Sleepy Duskywing, *Erynnis brizo*
Mournful Duskywing, *Erynnis tristis* (probably)

California Black Oak, *Quercus kelloggii*

California Sister, *Adelpha bredowii californica*

Scrub Live Oak, *Quercus wislizeni*
var *frutescens*

Gold-hunter's Hairstreak, *Satyrium auretorum*
California Hairstreak, *Satyrium californica*
California Sister, *Adelpha bredowii californica*
Mournful Duskywing, *Erynnis tristis*

PEA FAMILY, FABACEAE
Catclaw, *Acacia greggii*

Marine Blue, *Leptotes marina*
Reakirt's Blue, *Hemiargus isola*
Ceraunus Blue, *Hemiargus ceraunus*

False Indigo, *Amorpha fruticosa*

California Dogface, *Zerene eurydice*
Marine Blue, *Leptotes marina*
Northern Cloudywing, *Thorybes pylades*

Desert Rattlepod, *Astragalus crotalariae*

Orange Sulphur, *Colias eurytheme*
Ceraunus Blue, *Hemiargus ceraunus*

Parish Locoweed, *Astragalus douglasii*
var *parishii*

Harford's Sulphur, *Colias harfordii*
Ceraunus Blue, *Hemiargus ceraunus*
Western Tailed Blue, *Everes amyntula*
Silvery Blue, *Glaucopsyche lygdamus australis*
Melissa Blue, *Lycaeides melissa*

Palmer Locoweed, *Astragalus palmeri*

Harford's Sulphur, *Colias harfordii*
Ceraunus Blue, *Hemiargus ceraunus*
Western Tailed Blue, *Everes amyntula*

Nevada Lotus, *Lotus nevadensis*

Acmon Blue, *Plebejus acmon*
Melissa Blue, *Lycaeides melissa* (probably)
Afranius Duskywing, *Erynnis afranius*

119

Spanish Clover, *Lotus purshianus*

Acmon Blue, *Plebejus acmon*
Melissa Blue, *Lycaeides melissa*
Afranius Duskywing, *Erynnis afranius*

Desert Lotus, *Lotus rigidus*

Silvery Blue, *Glaucopsyche lygdamus australis*

Deerweed, *Lotus scoparius*

Orange Sulphur, *Colias eurytheme*
Harford's Sulphur, *Colias harfordii*
Bramble Hairstreak, *Callophrys perplexa*
Gray Hairstreak, *Strymon melinus*
Marine Blue, *Leptotes marina*
Silvery Blue, *Glaucopsyche lygdamus australis*
Acmon Blue, *Plebejus acmon*
Funereal Duskywing, *Erynnis funeralis*

Bishop Lotus, *Lotus strigosus*

Orange Sulphur, *Colias eurytheme*
Bramble Hairstreak, *Callophrys perplexa*
Acmon Blue, *Plebejus acmon*

Arizona Lupine, *Lupinus arizonicus*

Painted Lady, *Vanessa cardui*

Miniature Lupine, *Lupinus bicolor*

Orange Sulphur, *Colias eurytheme*
Acmon Blue, *Plebejus acmon*

Grape Soda Lupine, *Lupinus excubitus*

Silvery Blue, *Glaucopsyche lygdamus australis*
Boisduval's Blue, *Plebejus icarioides evius*
Melissa Blue, *Lycaeides melissa*

Adonis Lupine, *Lupinus formosus*

Silvery Blue, *Glaucopsyche lygdamus australis*
Arrowhead Blue, *Glaucopsyche piasus umbrosa*
Boisduval's Blue, *Plebejus icarioides evius*

Desert Ironwood, *Olneya tesota*

Funereal Duskywing, *Erynnis funeralis*

Honey Mesquite, *Prosopis glandulosa*

Leda Ministreak, *Ministrymon leda*
Marine Blue, *Leptotes marina*
Reakirt's Blue, *Hemiargus isola*
Ceraunus Blue, *Hemiargus ceraunus*
Palmer's Metalmark, *Apodemia palmeri*

Screwbean Mesquite, *Prosopis pubescens*

Marine Blue, *Leptotes marina* (probably)
Reakirt's Blue, *Hemiargus isola*
Ceraunus Blue, *Hemiargus ceraunus*
Palmer's Metalmark, *Apodemia palmeri*

Indigobush, *Psorothamnus schottii*

Painted Lady, *Vanessa cardui*

Desert Cassia, *Senna armata*

Sleepy Orange, *Eurema nicippe*
Cloudless Sulphur, *Phoebis sennae*
Gray Hairstreak, *Strymon melinus*

Coues' Cassia, *Senna covesii*

Sleepy Orange, *Eurema nicippe*
Cloudless Sulphur, *Phoebis sennae*

PLANTAIN FAMILY, PLANTAGINACEAE
Woolly Plantain, *Plantago ovata*

Painted Lady, *Vanessa cardui*

120

Southwestern Plantain, *Plantago patagonica* — Quino Checkerspot, *Euphydryas editha quino*
Common Buckeye, *Junonia coenia*

ROSE FAMILY, ROSACEAE
Chamise, *Adenostoma fasciculatum* — Brown Elfin, *Callophrys augustinus*
Marine Blue, *Leptotes marina*
Spring Azure, *Celastrina ladon echo*

Mountain-Mahogany, *Cercocarpus betuloides* — California Hairstreak, *Satyrium californica*
Mountain Mahogany Hairstreak, *Satyrium tetra*

Cleveland's Horkelia, *Horkelia clevelandii* — 'Laguna' Two-banded Checkered-Skipper, *Pyrgus ruralis lagunae*

Hollyleaf Cherry, *Prunus ilicifolia* — Pale Swallowtail, *Papilio eurymedon*
Brown Elfin, *Callophrys augustinus*
Spring Azure, *Celastrina ladon echo*

Western Chokecherry, *Prunus virginiana* — Pale Swallowtail, *Papilio eurymedon*
California Hairstreak, *Satyrium californica*
Lorquin's Admiral, *Limenitis lorquini*

SNAPDRAGON FAMILY, SCROPHULARIACEAE
White Snapdragon, *Antirrhinum coulterianum* — Quino Checkerspot, *Euphydryas editha quino*
Common Buckeye, *Junonia coenia*

Purple Owl's Clover, *Castilleja exserta* — Quino Checkerspot, *Euphydryas editha quino*
Common Buckeye, *Junonia coenia*

Woolly Indian Paintbrush, *Castilleja foliolosa* — Leanira Checkerspot, *Chlosyne leanira wrighti*
'Henne' Variable Checkerspot, *Euphydryas chalcedona hennei*

Desert Bushpenstemon, *Keckiella antirrhinoides* — 'Henne' Variable Checkerspot, *Euphydryas chalcedona hennei*

Seep Monkeyflower, *Mimulus guttatus* — Mylitta Crescent, *Phyciodes mylitta*

STONECROP FAMILY, CRASSULACEAE
Desert Dudleya, *Dudleya saxosa* — Gray Hairstreak, *Strymon melinus*
Sonoran Blue, *Philotes sonorensis*

SUNFLOWER FAMILY, ASTERACEAE
Desert Goldenhead, *Acamptopappus sphaerocephalus* — 'Neumoegen's' Sagebrush Checkerspot, *Chlosyne acastus neumoegeni*

San Felipe Dyssodia, *Adenophyllum porophylloides* — Dainty Sulphur, *Nathalis iole*

Mulefat, *Baccharis salicifolia* — Spring Azure, *Celastrina ladon echo*

Sweetbush, *Bebbia juncea* — Wright's Metalmark, *Calephelis wrighti*

Thistles, *Cirsium* spp — Mylitta Crescent, *Phyciodes mylitta*
Painted Lady, *Vanessa cardui*

121

Bird's Nest Thistle, *Cirsium scariosum*   Painted Lady, *Vanessa cardui*

Desert Dicoria, *Dicoria canescens*   Painted Lady, *Vanessa cardui*

Everlastings, *Gnaphalium* ssp   American Lady, *Vanessa virginiensis*

Sawtooth Goldenbush, *Hazardia squarrosa* ssp *grindelioides*   Gabb's Checkerspot, *Chlosyne gabbii*

Western Sunflower, *Helianthus annuus*   Gray Hairstreak, *Strymon melinus*
California Patch, *Chlosyne californica* (occasionally)
Bordered Patch, *Chlosyne lacinia crocale*

Cudweed Aster, *Lessingia filaginifolia*   Gabb's Checkerspot, *Chlosyne gabbii*

Spanish Needles, *Palafoxia arida*   Dainty Sulphur, *Nathalis iole*

Cinchweed, *Pectis papposa*   Dainty Sulphur, *Nathalis iole*

Parish Viguiera, *Viguiera parishii*   California Patch, *Chlosyne californica*
Bordered Patch, *Chlosyne lacinia crocale*

Orcutt's Aster, *Xylorhiza orcuttii*   'Neumoegen's' Sagebrush Checkerspot, *Chlosyne acastas neumoegeni*

SYCAMORE FAMILY, PLATANACEAE
California Sycamore, *Platanus racemosa*   Western Tiger Swallowtail, *Papilio rutulus*

VIOLET FAMILY, VIOLACEAE
Violets, *Viola* spp.   Variegated Fritillary, *Euptoieta claudia*

Mountain Violet, *Viola purpurea*   Callippe Fritillary, *Speyeria callippe comstocki*
Coronis Fritillary, *Speyeria coronis semiramis*

WILLOW FAMILY, SALICACEAE
Fremont Cottonwood, *Populus fremontii*   Mourning Cloak, *Nymphalis antiopa*

Willows, *Salix* spp   California Hairstreak, *Satyrium californica*
Gray Hairstreak, *Strymon melinus*
Lorquin's Admiral, *Limenitis lorquini*

Slender Willow, *Salix exigua*   Western Tiger Swallowtail, *Papilio rutulus*
Sylvan Hairstreak, *Satyrium silvinus*
Mourning Cloak, *Nymphalis antiopa*
Lorquin's Admiral, *Limenitis lorquini* (probably)

Largeleaf Willow, *Salix laevigata*   Lorquin's Admiral, *Limenitis lorquini* (probably)

Arroyo Willow, *Salix lasiolepis*   Western Tiger Swallowtail, *Papilio rutulus*
Sylvan Hairstreak, *Satyrium silvinus*
Lorquin's Admiral, *Limenitis lorquini*

References
Butterflies and their Caterpillar Food Plants
Asterisks indicate references used as sources for the caterpillar food plants

*Ballmer, G. R., and G. F. Pratt. 1988. "A survey of the last instar larvae of the Lycaenidae of California." *Journal of Research on the Lepidoptera,* 27 (1): 1–81.

Barth, F. G. (translated by M. A. Biederman-Thorson). 1991. *Insects and Flowers: The Biology of a Partnership.* Princeton, NJ: Princeton University Press.

Brock, J. P., and K. Kaufman. 2003. *Butterflies of North America.* New York: Houghton Mifflin.

*Brown, J. W., H. G. Real, and D. K. Faulkner. 1992. *Butterflies of Baja California.* Beverly Hills, CA: Lepidoptera Research Foundation.

Dameron, W. 1997. *Searching for Butterflies in Southern California.* Los Angeles: Flutterby Press.

Dice, J., J. Brown and D. Hillyard, compilers. 1998. *Butterflies Recorded from the Sentenac Canyon Area.* Anza-Borrego Foundation: Sentenac Canyon Field Trip. Unpublished.

Ehrlich, P. R. and P. H. Raven. 1964. "Butterflies and plants: a study in coevolution." *Evolution,* 18: 586–608.

Ehrlich, P. R. and P. H. Raven. 1967 "Butterflies and plants." *Scientific American,* 216: 105–113.

*Emmel, J., and G. Pratt. 2003. "2002 Season Summary," *News of the Lepidopterists' Society,* 45: supplement S1, p. 13.

Emmel, J. F., and T. C. Emmel. 1998. "A New Subspecies of the Giant Skipper *Megathymus yuccae* from San Diego County, California (Lepidoptera: Hesperiidae: Megathyminae)" in T. C. Emmel, Ed. *Systematics of Western North American Butterflies.* Gainesville, FL: Mariposa Press, pp. 763–766.

*Emmel, J. F., T. C. Emmel and S. O. Mattoon. 1998. "New Polyommatinae Subspecies of Lycaenidae (Lepidoptera) from California" in T. C. Emmel, Ed. *Systematics of Western North American Butterflies.* Gainesville, FL: Mariposa Press, pp. 171–200.

*Emmel, J. F., T. C. Emmel and S. O. Mattoon. 1998. "New Subspecies of Pieridae (Lepidoptera) from California, Nevada, and Baja California" in T. C. Emmel, Ed. *Systematics of Western North American Butterflies.* Gainesville, FL: Mariposa Press, pp. 127–138.

*Emmel, J. F., T. C. Emmel and G. F. Pratt. 1998. "Five new subspecies of *Apodemia mormo* (Lepidoptera: Riodinidae) from Southern California" in T. C. Emmel, Ed. *Systematics of Western North American Butterflies.* Gainesville, FL: Mariposa Press, pp. 801–810.

Emmel, T. C., Ed. 1998. *Systematics of Western North American Butterflies.* Gainesville, FL: Mariposa Press.

*Emmel, T. C., and J. F. Emmel. 1973. *The Butterflies of Southern California.* Natural History Museum of Los Angeles County, Science Series no. 26.

*Garth, J. S., and J. W. Tilden. 1986. *California Butterflies.* California Natural History Guide 51. Berkeley: University of California Press.

Glassberg, J. 2001. *Butterflies Through Binoculars: The West, A Field Guide to the Butterflies of Western North America.* New York: Oxford University Press.

Heath, F. and H. Clarke. 2003. *An Introduction to Southern California Butterflies.* Missoula, MT: Mountain Press Publishing Company.

Heppner, J. B. 1971 (1973). The distribution of *Paratrytone melane* and its spread into San Diego County (Hesperiidae). *Journal of Research on the Lepidoptera,* 10 (4): 287–300.

Levy, J. N. 1998. "Definitive Destination: Anza-Borrego Desert State Park, California." *American Butterflies,* 6 (1): 4–15.

Nijhout, H. F. 1991. *The Development and Evaluation of Butterfly Wing Patterns.* Washington DC and London: Smithsonian Institute Press.

North American Butterfly Association (NABA) Checklist & *English Names of North American Butterflies.* 1995. Morristown, NJ: North American Butterfly Association.

*Opler, P. O. 1999. *A Field Guide to Western Butterflies,* 2nd Ed. Boston: Houghton Mifflin Co.

Opler, P. O. and A. D. Warren. 2002. *Butterflies of North America. 2. Scientific Names List for Butterfly Species of North America, North of Mexico.* Contributions of the C. P. Gillette Museum of Arthropod Diversity. Fort Collins, CO: Colorado State University

Personal communications: *G. Ballmer; J. Emmel; D. Faulkner; J. Oliver; P. Opler; K. Osborne; *G. Pratt; J. Scott; R. Stanford.

*Pratt, G. F. and J. F. Emmel. 1998. "Revision of the *Euphilotes enoptes* and *E. battoides* complexes (Lepidoptera: Lycaenidae)" in T. C. Emmel, Ed. *Systematics of Western North American Butterflies.* Gainesville, FL: Mariposa Press, pp. 207–270.

Prudic, K. L., A. M. Shapiro, and N. S. Clayton. 2001. "Evaluating a putative mimetic relationship between two butterflies, *Adelpha bredowii* and *Limenitis lorquini.*" *Ecological Entomology,* 27: 68–75.

Pyle, R. M. 1981. *The Audubon Society Field Guide to North American Butterflies.* New York: Chanticleer Press.

*Scott, J. A. 1986. *The Butterflies of North America: A Natural History and Field Guide.* Stanford, CA: Stanford University Press.

Stanford, R. E., R. L. Langston, and K. Davenport, compilers. 2002. *Early/Late California Butterfly Records,* 16th revision. Unpublished.

Stanford, R. E., and P. A. Opler. 1993. *Atlas of Western USA Butterflies.* Denver: Privately published.

Stewart, B. 1997. *Common Butterflies of California.* Point Reyes Station, CA: West Coast Lady Press.

Tilden, J. W., and A. C. Smith. 1986. *A Field Guide to Western Butterflies.* Boston: Houghton Mifflin Co.

Plants

Asterisks indicate references used as sources for the caterpillar food plants

*Beauchamp, R. M. 1986. *A Flora of San Diego County, California.* National City, CA: Sweetwater River Press.

*Clemons, D., compiler. 1986. *Plants of Anza-Borrego Desert State Park.* Borrego Springs, CA: Anza-Borrego Desert Natural History Association.

Crampton, B. 1974. *Grasses in California.* California Natural History Guides 33. Berkeley: University of California Press.

Hickman, J. C., Ed. 1993. *The Jepson Manual: Higher Plants of California.* Berkeley: University of California Press.

Johnson, Paul R. 1982. *Cacti, Shrubs and Trees of Anza-Borrego: An Amateur's Key for Identifying Desert Plants.* Borrego Springs, CA: Anza-Borrego Desert Natural History Association.

McMinn, H. E. 1939. *An Illustrated Manual of California Shrubs.* Berkeley: University of California Press.

Munz, P. A. 1974. *A Flora of Southern California.* Berkeley: University of California Press.

*Reiser, C. Personal communications regarding several food plant identifications.

The Xerces Society and The Smithsonian Institution. 1998. *Butterfly Gardening: Creating Summer Magic in Your Garden.* San Francisco: Sierra Club Books

Index to Caterpillar Food Plants & Selected Nectar Plants

Also see "Caterpillar Food Plants and Butterfly Species," pp. 114–122.

Caterpillar Food Plants: indexed by common names, genus/species and families; numbers in normal type; food plants with pictures have numbers **bolded.**

Nectar Plants: all those pictured are indexed by common names and genus/species; numbers in *italics.*

Note: Caterpillar Food Plant entries precede Nectar Plant entries, separated by a semi-colon.

Index to Butterflies

Also see "Butterflies & their Caterpillar Food Plants," pp. 106–113.
Butterflies are indexed by common name, genus, species, subspecies, families and subfamilies.
The main entry for each butterfly has a **bolded** page number.

About the Authors

The authors are avid naturalists with a special interest in the smaller creatures. As full-time residents in Borrego Springs in 1990–1991 after careers in education and dentistry, they became intrigued with the extraordinary plants and animals of this region, especially its many butterflies and other insects. In 1990 they trained as naturalists in the Canyoneers Program at the San Diego Natural History Museum. Subsequently, as part-time residents they have carried on field studies of the plants and insects. Since 1997 they have conducted annual NABA (North American Butterfly Association) butterfly counts in Anza-Borrego Desert State Park® and environs. The authors are members of the Lepidopterists Society, the North American Butterfly Association and the Xerces Society.

Lynn, a college English teacher with a special interest in native plants, has written many articles on flowers and gardens. Gene, a geologist/mineralogist and dentist, served on the faculty of the State University of NY, College of Ceramic Engineering and has numerous publications in the fields of biomedical materials and mineralogy. Together they authored *Sonnenberg Garden* (1985), a photographic guide. Several of their garden and plant photographs were selected for inclusion in *Gardens of America: Three Centuries of Design* (1989). This is their first book on butterflies.

About the Photographs

This book contains 480 photographs by the authors, almost all taken in natural undisturbed conditions in the wild. Where no natural photos were available, museum specimens, provided courtesy of Dr. Paisley Cato, Curator at the San Diego Natural History Museum and Virginia Scott, Collections Manager at the University of Colorado, were photographed. In addition, six botanical drawings of plant species were used.

These illustrations include:

286 butterfly photos including 87 sipping flowers and 31 on caterpillar food plants
48 photos of immature stages—egg, caterpillar and chrysalis
146 photos and 6 color drawings of caterpillar food plants and butterfly nectar plants

Photographs were taken with Nikon cameras using a 105 mm Nikkor micro lens or a Sigma 70–300 mm macro lens on Kodak Professional Ektachrome E100S.

Front cover photo: *Desert Agaves in Mason Valley looking west to the Peninsular Range*
Insert: *California Giant-Skipper on Desert Agave, its caterpillar food plant*
Back cover photo: *Leanira Checkerspot sipping Narrowleaf Goldenbush*